Hounds Creek Chronicles

Eldridge Bagley

ELDRIDGE BAGLEY

Cover art by
Eldridge Bagley

Acknowledgements

My sister, Ann Bagley Hancock, and my brother, Grayson Hardie Bagley, helped create many priceless memories during our growing up years together. I am grateful to them for that, and for their enthusiasm in sharing their personal recollections with me as I worked on this project. I would like to thank my wife Beth for her encouragement and for patiently sharing her computer knowledge and skills as I prepared the text. Thanks to my brother-in-law, Herman Hancock, for his help in gathering details regarding the music of the times. I want to express my appreciation to Susan Lenhart for her valued work in editing the manuscript. Finally, thanks to Francis and Chris Wood for their input and encouragement as I prepared for publication, and to Jon Marken and Dan Dwyer at Farmville Printing for their help and guidance in the design and printing of this book.

Dedicated to the memory of my parents,
Waverly and Patsy Bagley.

Table of Contents

Preface

*I*t was a bitterly cold January evening in 2003, and the night air was unusually crisp. The sky glittered with stars and patches of snow lay randomly on the frozen ground. As I walked through the yard of the house where I had grown up, I could hear Hounds Creek making its continuous journey over rocks acres away. Then, another sound, unlike any that I recalled hearing before, pierced the night and caused me to stop in my tracks. I considered that a large chunk of snow might have slid off a nearby roof and crashed to the ground, but the noise seemed to have come from somewhere down in a distant pasture. It puzzled me, but I moved on and soon forgot about it.

Some days later as I was walking through the lower pastures, I discovered what had caused the mysterious crashing sound. The old log striproom that my father had built as a young man in the 1930's had collapsed and lay on the ground, a tangled wreck of weathered wood and tin. The building that we once used for preparing tobacco for market had deteriorated through the years, and I knew that its demise was inevitable. It saddened me though to see it now in the light of a winter morning, a mere pile of useless rubble. The striproom was significant to our family, not only because of the practical purposes it had served, but also because of all the memories that were attached to it—memories of our farming years. It would now return to the earth, just as our stable and barn had done years earlier. The incident underscored for me the fact that time changes things, and in the process we often lose touch with places and people that have played a significant part in shaping our lives.

I have observed firsthand the passing of a way of life that both nurtured and challenged those who lived it. The real purpose of this book is to offer a close look at a lifestyle that seemed rather ordinary at the time, but one that has turned out to be quite remarkable after all.

Introduction

Streams of flowing water are living things, and I have always regarded them with a sense of awe and awareness that each stream possesses its own unique characteristics. Whether a tiny branch meandering through a pasture or a sizable river rushing toward the sea, streams seem to parallel human life in some ways. The big difference between the parallel journeys, of course, is that streams do not know where they came from or remember where they have been. They are not aware of their destination, and they don't really have a choice in the matter. They follow a course long ago determined, and within the general confines of that course they will remain. Not necessarily so with humans. We *can* know where we began life. We *can* recall our journey to the present and, to some extent, chart the course we wish to follow for the remainder of it. It is *awareness* of our surroundings that makes our journey meaningful to us.

As one who has lived all of his life in the same place, I find that my awareness of my surroundings has grown significantly over time. While for some people the idea of viewing life from a consistent vantage point might seem to offer a limited perspective and no journey at all, I have found the opposite to be true. I have been able to gain some revealing insights into the human experience as I have observed the ebb and flow of daily life around me. The natural cycles that constitute the living out of one's days on this earth have become apparent. The certainty and consistency of birth, growth, vitality, maturity, decline, and death in the lives of people that I have known for so long have confirmed for me that those cycles are in place by grand design. Farmers often observe this ebb and flow as reflected in the life of a plant. A kernel of corn dropped into the cultivated earth sprouts, develops into a sturdy stalk, yields grain, and eventually dies. It leaves behind the seeds necessary for new life to emerge, and the cycle is repeated.

Thinking back to the respective journeys of streams and humans, we realize how vastly varied those journeys can be. My personal journey has not been like that of a surging river that sweeps past a dramatically changing landscape. It has been more like that of a small creek that winds through familiar territory, with an intimate knowledge of the coves and shallows, the twists and turns, and of the seasonal cycles that surround them. The origins of that journey were being formed during the years that preceded my birth, and that is where *Hounds Creek Chronicles* begins.

Pioneers on Poorhouse Road

*I*n early 1934, with the country mired in the Great Depression, my father was looking to buy some land. He was still living at home and farming with his parents near Kenbridge, Virginia, but he hoped to marry soon, and he wanted a farm of his own. About that time a small farm several miles from Kenbridge was put up for auction. On that forty acre tract stood a weathered three-room house, a log tobacco barn, and a stable. The land was poor and largely covered with scrub pines, gullies, and broomstraw. However, my father needed land, and I suppose that he had a vision of what the farm could become.

When my father approached the auction site that January morning, it must have been with some degree of trepidation. The public auction was to be held in front of the Bank of Lunenburg in Kenbridge. At the age of twenty-two, he was a young man with stout hopes, but a thin wallet. The truth is that most folks were in dire straits at the time. It is a tribute to my father's vision and resolve that when the auction was over, the run-down little farm was his. Many years later he would recall that he placed one final bid that morning, knowing that it would have to be his last. No one topped his bid, and Daddy's purchase of that particular farm in the community of Plymouth would have a profound impact on the lives of my parents, their children, and even their grandchildren for the rest of their lives.

My parents met when my mother visited relatives who

lived on land adjoining the farm where my Bagley grandparents lived. Waverly Eldridge Bagley and Patsy Wilson Hardie were married on December 6, 1934, in Graham, North Carolina where my mother's folks lived. The marriage took place at five-thirty a.m. in the Methodist parsonage, with only a couple of relatives present as attendants. Getting married at that hour enabled my parents to get an early start on their wedding trip, which took them into Virginia and included a visit to Natural Bridge. After that brief trip, they returned to the forty-acre farm to begin their life together. For my father, I suppose the acres of rolling land held great promise. For my mother, who had been living in a fairly sizable town, the farm may have appeared rather desolate and lonely. My parents were somewhat latter-day pioneers as they settled into the Plymouth Community in the 1930's. Only a few homesteads had been established along Poorhouse Road at that time and most of the folks living there were tobacco farmers. The road got its name from the fact that a poorhouse had once stood nearby.

The old house into which Mother and Daddy moved was nowhere near the main road, but situated on the backside of the farm a short distance from the creek. There was one large room downstairs and two smaller ones upstairs. The structure sat upon stone pillars, had never been painted, and had been without tenants for several years. With no underpinning, frigid winter winds swept beneath its floors, sometimes causing the thin linoleum rugs to flap up and down. The only heat sources were a wood-burning tin heater and a cook-stove, and the cracked plaster walls had no insulation. The dwelling offered basic shelter, and my parents lived there for more than ten years with no electricity, bathroom, or running water. Kerosene lamps provided light, and a bold spring located several hundred feet down the hill served as their source of water. Mother used the spring to cool stews and other foods that she had cooked and prepared to pour into canning jars. After my sister Ann was born, Mother also placed bottles of baby formula there to prevent spoilage. Occasionally my father would bring home a big block of ice from the icehouse in Kenbridge, but that was a luxury rarely afforded.

My parents had a battery-operated radio in the house and that was the only means for bringing in entertainment from the outside world. There was no telephone. It would not be long before electricity and telephones would be enjoyed even in the most remote areas. However, for various reasons, not the least of which was financial, many farm families in the area would not avail themselves of those services until years down the road.

A very large cedar tree stood beside the house, and Adirondack chairs were practically permanent fixtures within its shade. My parents would sit there on summer evenings after days of strenuous work and claim a brief respite from their labors as they watched my sister at play. That time and place marked the beginning of a long and rugged road that my parents would navigate together.

Soon after Mother and Daddy settled onto their newly acquired land, an elderly neighbor lady who was familiar with the farm was heard to remark: "Poor Waverly and Patsy—they'll never be able to make a livin' on that red land." Some folks might not have, but my parents were committed—to each other and to making a living and raising a family. They also possessed a substantial capacity for hard work. Ever so slowly, as the seasons passed, Mother and Daddy transformed the neglected

My parents, Waverly and Patsy Bagley in the 1930's.

farm into a productive and somewhat profitable one. My father cut trees with an axe and—with help on the other end—a crosscut saw. He plowed, limed, fertilized, and terraced to restore the nutrient-deprived soil. He practiced crop rotation and sought the help of the local county agent and other advisers in managing the land that he worked and loved. Mother often worked in the fields too, putting in long days of intensive labor in addition to her household responsibilities.

Not having been around at that time, I have tried to imagine what life was really like for my parents and my sister at that old house and what the close of day might have brought to that setting. On moonlit nights, the house must have loomed as a towering silhouette. No doubt, a dim light appeared each evening in an upstairs window as my mother lit a kerosene lamp and put my sister to bed. When the old building finally became dark and silent, it must have cast a long shadow across the yard and the well-worn path that led to the front door. In the summer my parents probably drifted off to sleep amid a soft symphony of night sounds like the ones that I hear when I revisit the site on a summer evening.

The New House

Farmers often constructed their own buildings, either by themselves or with help from family and neighbors. By 1944 my parents were making plans to build a new house, and later that year Daddy enlisted a couple of his brothers to help him with the job. They selected and cut trees from my parents' farm, delivered them to a local sawmill, and had them sawn into lumber. Using skills they had honed while putting up farm buildings and helping to construct military barracks at Camp Pickett several years earlier, they built my parents a modest, but attractive, home. The chosen site was on the front portion of the farm, still well off the main road, but much closer than the old house had been. My mother helped draw plans for the house that included the large kitchen she wanted and dormer windows. This major project of building a home from scratch had to be wedged in-between farm work, and that meant doing the job in stages — and as finances allowed. By the late spring of 1945, the downstairs rooms had been completed, and my parents moved in about six months before I was born. During the next several years, my father finished the upstairs rooms.

There must have been quite a contrast between life in a drafty old house near the creek and a bright, new home on a ridge that offered my folks a view of the main road and several other houses. From the north windows of their new house, they could catch a glimpse of their growing community. After a decade of kerosene lamps and toting water from a spring, the convenience of electricity at last brought welcomed changes to my parents' home life. My uncle and aunt, Harris and Lucy Bagley, had married and settled on the adjoining farm in the late 1930's—about the same time that the Walkers and Spencers settled across the road. Soon the Dodson, Stables, and Spruill families would establish homes nearby, and others would eventually follow. Within a couple of decades, my parents would be able to stand in their front yard and see the lights from a dozen homes. As the community continued to grow, strong bonds that would last for a lifetime began to form between the neighbors.

To Know the Land

*B*ecause farmers live intimately with the land that they work, it follows that they should know it well and understand the nature of it. My father did. He had already learned a great deal from his father while growing up and working on his parents' farm with his six brothers. He learned still more through laboring and coaxing crops from his own farm. It soon became apparent to him that the front acreage was red, poor, and starved for lime. The middle acreage was a little less clay-like, and the lower fields became sandier as they sloped toward the creek. The red clay was hard, but it held moisture well. The sandy soil was easy to work, but moisture slipped through it like water through a sieve. As Daddy combined the knowledge that he had gleaned from Grandpa Bagley and the local farm office with his own experimentation, the land finally began to yield the results he had believed were possible.

Farmers—at least small farmers with limited land— had a curious tendency to employ descriptive phrases when referring to various parts of their farms. Other members of the family would adopt those terms, and the phrases became a part of the family's personal colloquialism. Even after all these years, my siblings and I know that "the long field" refers to a long, narrow strip of land near the creek on the southwest portion of the farm. The "mule pasture" was a triangular plot with a deep ravine at its center. Assorted refuse had been deposited there years before—including the rusty remains of a Model T. That pasture was reserved primarily for our team of mules. The "new ground" was a small clearing of rocky soil, reclaimed from young trees and brush, and we grew tobacco there in the latter years of our farming.

And so it was understood among rural folks that each farm possessed certain characteristics that gave it a peculiar nature—a "personality" of sorts. That nature would come to be thoroughly known by the farm's owners and rediscovered by new owners when the farm changed hands.

Trail of Tears
And Other Recollections of Tobacco

*T*obacco was our chief money crop when I was growing up and, I might add, the chief stress producer. Tobacco farm families developed their own vocabulary to describe countless challenges that faced them throughout the year. Some of those challenges hovered like dark clouds on a summer horizon, issuing vague warnings like the ominous rumble of distant thunder. During the growing and harvesting season especially, there was a steady stream of concerns that would have defeated a less hardy breed of folks. Drought, hailstorms, windstorms, relentless rains, blue mold, tobacco worms, aphids, DDT and other pesticides, wiregrass, crabgrass, blank shank (wilt), sunburn, heat exhaustion, barns lost to fire, ornery mules, aging tractors, and, finally, the ever-changing whims of tobacco buyers—all these and more combined to take a heavy toll on the tobacco farmer and his family. No wonder the faces of tobacco farmers became leathery and careworn years earlier than they should have. No wonder farmers and their families were so tough—they *had* to be in order to survive. The farm men and women that I knew were a robust lot. There was little tolerance for whining. Every farmer's kid, including myself, had to learn that.

For those who actually enjoyed the rigors of tobacco farming in the 1950's, there was plenty to enjoy. Even though I could never quite grasp how anyone could find pleasure in suckering tobacco, I did come to understand that there is a certain intangible satisfaction that rewards the days of labor spent in sweltering fields.

If a tobacco farmer's son or daughter began their working years on the farm thinking that work could be caught up and there would be periods of leisure, those notions were soon dispelled. My view of tobacco quickly became one of thinly veiled disdain for a crop that demanded relentless and intense labor. Tobacco was a harsh taskmaster, and one with which I became well acquainted early in life. My older sister Ann and my younger brother Grayson and I were initiated into the rite of "handing leaves" by the time we were eight or nine years old.

The methods that my family used in growing tobacco were similar to those employed by other farm families. The initial work for production of a tobacco crop began in January with the preparation of land for plant patches—plots for the sowing of tobacco seeds. By early spring those seeds were young plants that needed to be watered and weeded repeatedly. We dipped buckets of water by hand from a branch, filling several large barrels, and then hauled them by trailer to the plant patches. There we repeated the process in reverse, emptying the barrels one bucket at a time and soaking the patches thoroughly. When it was time to weed, we each took an assigned portion of the plant bed and on hands and knees pulled up every sprig of grass and every weed by its roots. It was a tedious and time consuming process, but necessary for the sustained growth of the tobacco plants. Plant beds were protected from frost by a thin canvas, which was spread over the bed and attached to small logs around the perimeter. The watering and weeding of plant patches continued at intervals until the plants were ready to transplant.

Farmers in southern Virginia prepared their fields in April, and by early May it was time to plant tobacco. Plants were pulled by hand early in the morning, when possible, and carefully packed into crates and boxes. Guano bags saturated with water were laid over the crated plants to keep them fresh. Tobacco farmers were still using hand planters in the 1950's. The process required two people: one to operate the planter

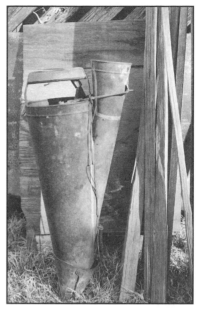

The hand-operated tobacco planter was a familiar and important piece of equipment on tobacco farms when I was growing up.

and one to drop the plants into the planter. Callus built up on top of callus. During planting season, there was little question concerning what awaited my sister and my brother and me when we got home from school. There would be a change of clothes, a quick snack, and a prompt appearance at the dusty fields where our parents had been planting all day. Those afternoons would be long ones, filled with toting water and dropping tobacco plants.

As summer arrived in full force, tobacco required even more of our attention. On good years the plants grew tall and eventually flowered out at the top into clusters of pink and white blooms. This was no romantic bouquet. Breaking that cluster of flowers from the top of the plant was necessary to force growth into the leaves. Farmers referred to the process as "topping," and it prompted the growth of suckers at the base of almost every leaf. Suckers impaired leaf growth, so they had to be dealt with. During those years, farmers used mineral oil to fight suckers. After breaking off the top of the plant, a small amount of oil was squirted from a hand held oilcan. As the oil slowly ran down the stalk, it penetrated many of the tender suckers, gradually stifling their growth. Some of the suckers escaped the oil and grew with abandon. They had to be removed, and that led to the most hated, the most reviled job in the life of a farmer's kid—suckering. To sucker was to walk up and down every row in every field and remove every sucker from every plant—top to bottom. My father's watchful eye would not overlook slovenly work, especially when it came to tobacco. The knowledge of that fact was enough to discourage us from skipping suckers, however much we might have wanted to. Besides, if we skipped suckers, they would only be that much bigger and tougher the following week when we repeated the process all over again. Suckering took place during the most intense heat that summer had to offer, and it was the perfect set-up for heat exhaustion. We experienced it numerous times—the nausea, the vomiting, and the dehydration that left us too weak to do anything but lie upon the sofa or beneath the shade of a tree. By late August, most of the suckering was behind us and considered a good riddance.

During my growing up years, the majority of farmers, including my father, cured tobacco with wood. Our wood-cutting began in the winter as we felled trees to clear land for plant patches and crops. The logs and saplings that we cut were placed in vertical stacks near each of our barns.

In anticipation of harvesting and curing the crop, June and early July were partially devoted to preparing the barns. It was dirty work. Smoky flues, their insides coated with layers of black soot, had to be put into place, fitted together, and stabilized. The problem was—they rarely *wanted* to fit together. Cracks in the furnace had to be filled. After pouring buckets of water into nearby mud holes, or in some cases, creating mud holes, we used garden hoes to work up a sizable batch of mud from the red clay soil. The mixture had a sensuous feel—warm and soupy—as we slung and pressed it by hand into every crack where mortar had fallen away. Finally, tobacco sticks, thermometers, stringers, and benches were all put into place, and by mid July everything was ready for the harvesting.

The Harvest

The most intense days of labor were still ahead as harvest season arrived. That process was commonly referred to as "pulling tobacco" or "saving leaves." Tobacco ripens from the bottom up, and by mid to late July, the leaves at the base of the plants began to yellow. Our crops would be harvested weekly as we worked our way up the stalk until the top leaves or "tips" were gathered in September.

Our "pulling" days usually began around 5:30 with breakfast before daylight. At the stable, the mule was bridled and hitched to a homemade slide, which consisted of a simple wooden frame covered with coarse fertilizer bags. Tobacco pullers filled the slide with armfuls of ripe leaves, and the mule pulled it to a bench where other workers took over. "Handers" gathered up bundles of leaves from the pile that had been carefully placed on a bench in front of them and passed them to the "stringer." Each bundle was expected to contain three leaves, no more and no less. While the handers were usually neighborhood kids, my mother and my sister did most of the stringing in the early years. The bundles were looped with twine onto long, splintery sticks and carefully laid in a bulk beside the barn door or in the shade of a tree. Later in the day, the sticks of heavy, and sometimes wet tobacco would be placed on tier poles inside the barn, high above the furnace and flues.

Working at the bench, usually beneath the hot tin roof of a barn shed, it was easy to become bored with the repetitive motion of handing bundles of leaves to the stringer. My thoughts wandered to the nearby fields where the pullers, who were a few years older than I, were working. I could hear voices bantering and shouting at the mule, accompanied by the cracking noise of brittle leaf stems being snapped from their stalks. I couldn't help but wonder if that might be a far more interesting place to work. When I became a teenager in the late 1950's, I graduated to the field. It was predominately a man's world out there — tough and almost hostile at times, owing to the nature of the work and to the work of Nature. There was no turning back, and the weight of the responsibilities that our parents would place upon my siblings and me would only increase in the years to follow.

For all the grueling labor though, there were some pleasurable moments. Stories and jokes were passed back and forth among the workers, both in the field and at the bench. We sang the latest hit songs and unveiled our future plans. Mother brought snacks to the barn that ranged from Popsicles to Moon Pies and Kool-Aid. Despite the fact that our hands were coated with thick layers of gummy, black tobacco wax, we savored every bite and enjoyed every gulp. The highlight of the day came when we gathered at midday for dinner around my parents' oak kitchen table. In front of tired, hungry workers, Mother placed dishes that included meat, mashed potatoes, black-eyed peas, baked tomatoes, corn pudding, candied yams, and fresh cobblers. After dinner, she returned to her place at the barn, and we reluctantly returned to ours.

Those sweltering summer days of tobacco harvesting may seem an unlikely place for strong bonds to form among family members and neighbors, but they did. There were meals and fellowship, but there was more. I have often considered why those bonds are so strong and why there is such an inclination to recall those hard, gritty days with a degree of fondness. Part of the answer may be just that. They *were* hard days. They were also *shared* days. We endured the struggles and the sweat together, and we survived them. Now we remember — and we celebrate.

The Curing

With harvesting underway, the curing process would follow. After a barn was filled, a fire was started in the furnace. Heat and smoke circulated through flues inside the barn and exited through a flue opening on the outside. A curing thermometer hung from a tier pole where it could be seen when the barn door was opened. There was an art to curing tobacco by this method, and tips on how best to do it were passed from parent to child. It was a process that could neither be rushed nor delayed, and it certainly could not be neglected. Both of my grandfathers had been tobacco farmers, and their generation believed that a fire must be maintained at all times during the course of curing. A round-the-clock fire required staying at the barn all night, catching naps between stoking the furnace, and sleeping on a bench or propped against a barn wall. By the time that I was old enough to remember, my father had relaxed that rule a bit. Still, I often watched him leave the house at night with a rusty lantern in his hand and head down a worn path to check on the barn fires. Occasionally he took his accordion, and later the strains of "Sweet Hour of Prayer" or some other familiar song would drift across the night air and through the screen door of the kitchen. During my teen years, I was frequently given the task of making sure that barn fires were well stoked for the night. Eventually my brother would be assigned the same task. I often sat on a log near the barn and watched the firelight as it cast an orange glow over the grass and the mounds of cold ashes nearby. It occurred to me that it would be a terrible thing to come down the path the next morning and find nothing but a pile of smoldering debris. There was always a risk that an untended barn could catch fire and burn. We never lost a barn, but a number of our neighbors did.

As curing proceeded, the temperature inside the barn increased daily, eventually reaching around 200 degrees. The final stage of curing required intense heat and was commonly referred to as "killing out a barn." The entire curing process took about a week. Properly cured tobacco would be crisp and, ideally, an appealing golden yellow. Things were often less than ideal though, and some tobacco of lesser quality cured up rough and discolored. Those problems would need to be dealt with later.

By the 1950's, we had three log tobacco barns on our farm. This barn was constructed around 1940 and is one of two that my father built, with help from neighbors.

Preparing for Market

As the steamy days of August melted away, a sense of anticipation took root in the hearts of the tobacco farmer and his family. With the approach of fall came the winding down of labor in fields of green tobacco. Attention turned to firing the last barns and preparing the year's harvest of cured leaves for market. Throughout the warm days and cooler nights of September, the aroma of curing tobacco blended with wood smoke from barn furnaces and wafted over pastures and fields of dried corn stalks.

Through the summer, as barns were emptied, we stored the cured tobacco in both the old house where my parents had once lived and in the "striproom." That term most likely originated in the days when whole stalks of tobacco were cured and leaves had to be stripped from the stalk to be prepared for market. My father had built the striproom in the 1930's. The floor was earthen, and tobacco was stored on a wooden platform along one side of the room until it could be tied. Just above head level stretched pine tier poles for hanging sticks of cured tobacco. In one corner a tin-covered steamer box sat upon a rock foundation. When water was poured into the box and a fire was started on the dirt floor beneath it, steam slowly filled the striproom and permeated the dry tobacco leaves, making them pliable for handling. A flue attached to the steam box carried smoke through a built-in chimney and into the air above the roof. One small northern window admitted light into the dark interior.

Work in the striproom usually involved at least two people. One person removed tobacco from the sticks, and another tied it into bundles. My mother tied most of our tobacco, gathering up a handful of leaves, carefully evaluating their quality, and tossing inferior leaves into a pile. This process of sorting was a crucial phase of preparing tobacco for the warehouse floor, where it would be critically examined by potential buyers and later auctioned. Discolored leaves, a little mold, or a few swelled stems—any of these could threaten the integrity of an entire batch of tobacco and cause buyers to back off. For all of these reasons and more, the person who tied tobacco ultimately had the responsibility of seeing that the finished product was acceptable and presented in the best possible way. From the bundle of leaves remaining in her hand after tossing discards, Mother selected the brightest, most supple leaf she could find. After folding it into a long narrow band, she wrapped the leaf around the head of the bundle, tucking the leaf stem into the middle of the bundle to secure it. Slowly and meticulously, she tied thousands of bundles. Later they would be hung on sticks, packed into the back of the pickup and transported to the warehouse.

During the tying process, the striproom's interior became covered with a layer of dirt and sand that had clung to tobacco leaves from the bottom of the plants. Dust and steam alternately filled the log room and gave it an almost ghostly appearance. But the mental images that I have retained of that time and place are crystal clear. I remember the darkened silhouettes of my parents quietly hovering over their work, enveloped within the thick fog that rose from the steamer. I can still see too, the cracked, tobacco-stained hands of my mother and father, doing their work with dignity, determination, and an acceptance that hard work was part and parcel of their life together.

The Market

The opening of the tobacco market heralded the final and most exciting phase of the farmer's crop year. This was precisely what he and his family had worked for, the goal toward which their rigorous labors had led. Not until years later did I realize how much was riding on auction day for my parents and other farmers like them. Would their tobacco, after all the care and pains they had taken, look good on the warehouse floor? Did the heavy summer rains produce tobacco that was too heavy and coarse? Had a drought left a crop that was immature and difficult to cure? Regardless of the price that tobacco might bring per pound, a light crop would not yield much income. And then the perennial question—what would the tobacco buyers want *this* year? Would it be orange, lemon yellow, or rusty brown? It mattered—a lot. There were fertilizer bills to pay off, school books to buy, and accounts due at the feed and seed store. Then too, this might be the year that the Kelvinator would choose to kick off, or the winter that the old Dodge pickup groaned its last.

The market opened earlier in North Carolina than in Virginia, and to get a jump on things, Daddy would sometimes book an early sale in Rocky Mount or Warrenton. For those trips we loaded the pickup the night before and carefully secured our cargo with a heavy brown wagon cover. Leaving in the darkness of early morning, we drove the approximately ninety miles and arrived at the warehouse shortly after daybreak. After unloading, we usually sought out a downtown restaurant for some breakfast. It was in those North Carolina towns that I tasted grits for the first time and decided that I had not missed much. Most of our tobacco was sold locally in Kenbridge. At the time, that town could boast of being the fourth largest tobacco market in Virginia, with five warehouses: The O.K., The Leader, Planters, Farmers, and The Dixie Lee.

As I remember, the same care and consideration given to preparing the tobacco for market at home was given to the leaves once they arrived at the warehouse. The bundles were gingerly removed from the sticks and placed upon flat, wooden baskets. The farmer or warehouse workers transported the baskets of tobacco to the scales for weighing, then placed them in rows alongside the tobacco of neighboring farmers.

When sale day finally arrived, parking space was at a premium in the warehouse "district" of Kenbridge. People came to the warehouses in droves. Farmers and their families mingled with buyers and warehousemen, filling the narrow aisles between tobacco rows. Neighbor visited with neighbor over endless piles of yellow harvest. The growing season, the weather, the crop, the family—all were topics of lively conversation. A rising drone of voices filled the huge warehouses as the sun streamed through skylights, revealing an almost carnival-like atmosphere. Finally, the call of the auctioneer crackled over a handheld loudspeaker and announced that the auction was about to begin. The hum of conversation subsided as attention turned to the main event. A crowd of faces, both fresh and weathered, both hopeful and apprehensive, moved up and down the rows between the tobacco piles. Sometimes jubilant, sometimes disappointed, occasionally frustrated, farmers usually had to accept what they were offered. There were times though, when my father and other farmers rejected the buyers' bids and requested that certain piles of their tobacco be offered again on another sale day.

Pleased or not, the tobacco farmer usually left the warehouse with at least some reward in his pocket and a list of businesses that were awaiting their share of that reward. Trying to stretch those modest earnings to make them last would be the next challenge. As the autumn afternoon waned and tobacco auctions came to an end, folks made their way up to Kenbridge's Broad Street or to Victoria to pay longstanding bills and to make the needed purchases that they had postponed for so long. Plans for the following year's crop were already taking shape in the minds of farmers, even as they stopped by the feed store to pay off their account balance and headed their battered old trucks in the direction of home.

In Grain

*I*t is either faith or foolishness that causes a farmer to plant thousands of corn kernels over acres of land, expecting something to happen. I believe it is the former. An astute farmer would not waste his time if he didn't believe that his efforts would produce a crop of grain. It requires hefty amounts of sweaty labor, along with huge investments of time, to take a crop from seeding to harvest. It also requires a miracle, and that's exactly what the farmer gets—the mysterious unfolding of new life from death, a vital, living plant from a hard "lifeless" kernel.

There was little doubt in our family that God provided the miracle part of every farm effort's success—the rain, the sun, the growth. If crops failed, and they sometimes did, we ultimately had to accept those failures as a hard reality of farm life.

Farmers in our area usually began planting corn around the tenth of April, when the leaves on trees were about the size of squirrels' ears. By the time the corn came up and started to grow, the danger of a killing frost would be past. Our days of corn planting began by lugging two-hundred-pound bags of fertilizer onto a trailer and hauling them to the field, where my father had prepared the rows days earlier. In the late 1950's, many farmers were still using mules to plant corn. The mule was bridled for an arduous day of plodding up and down the designated rows. Actually, pulling a corn planter was one of the easier jobs that a mule had to do, as the planter was lightweight and rolled on a single wheel.

The seeds that we poured into the planter had usually been purchased at Inge Feed and Seed, a local farmer's supply store in Kenbridge, and they were covered with a pink, powdery dust called Crow Tox. It was especially formulated to discourage those clever pests from pulling up the planted kernels or the sprouts that would soon emerge. It seemed to be a mild deterrent at best, and I sometimes wondered if the crows had actually developed a fondness for the stuff.

As the April sun rose higher above the southern Virginia landscape, highlighting splotches of white dogwood blossoms, the farmer and his mule slowly made their way across the cultivated fields. At the end of a long day, there was little to show for the effort except sunburned faces and blistered feet. How many miles did a farmer walk during a day of corn planting? As many as the mule could cover and the daylight would allow. I would like to say here how wonderful it felt to lie down and relax upon my bed before drifting off, but I don't remember anything about it. To lie down was to be gone—floating in a dreamless sleep.

Corn was not nearly as labor intensive a crop as tobacco though, especially during the summer months. Minimal chopping of weeds and cultivating kept it in pretty good shape. The real labor came along in September when the dried corn had to be cut and shucked. Armed with freshly sharpened corn knives and wearing long sleeve shirts to protect our arms from the rough corn leaves, we tackled the fields before us. We usually took two rows at a time, cutting and gathering up bundles of tall brittle stalks, then stacking them in shocks. Later we returned to shuck the corn, tossing the ears into a long trailer. As the trailer was pulled through autumn cornfields, it resembled a small pool of bright yellow moving through a vast sea of dull brown.

My father built our corncrib before I was born. Like many cribs of that era, the building was covered with tin and supported by tall cement posts, features that were supposed to make it rat proof. The final step in securing the corn harvest was to hand shovel each trailer load of corn onto the growing pile of yellow grain that was inside. Later the corn would be taken as needed to the mill in Kenbridge or Victoria, ground up, and mixed with supplements and molasses. The feed provided vital sustenance for our livestock.

Every aspect of farming contributed something to the richness and variety of a farm family's experiences. The sound of corn knives slicing through dried stalks and the aroma of the Corn Husker's Lotion that soothed our chapped hands pervade my memories of working in fields of golden grain.

Hay Days

*H*ay was never a primary crop on our farm, but it was an important one. In fact, it was the hay and various grains produced on our farm that carried our cows, sheep, hogs, and mules through severe winters and times of drought. Compared to contemporary standards, our hay harvesting methods would seem downright primitive. My father, like many other farmers, seldom had up-to-date equipment, and in the '30's and '40's, he cut hay with a horse-drawn mower. By the '50's, we were using a tractor-powered mower, although we were still using a mule to pull our hay rake. A row of long, curved "teeth" at the rear of the rake was raised and lowered by the use of a lever located beside the metal driver's seat. This rather curious contraption rolled on two large iron wheels that were joined to their hubs by spindly spokes.

Hay days provided more than we bargained for when we found ourselves racing a thunderstorm or when the mule happened to disturb a yellow jacket nest. But those times were exceptional. We loaded the raked hay by hand, using pitchforks with handles that were worn smooth as glass. The same method was used to unload. Profuse sweating served to plaster straw and chaff to our skin. Shafts of sunlight streamed through knotholes in the stable walls, revealing millions of dust particles—many of which found their way into our throats and nostrils. The last of the hay was put away by early October, and the fields rested for the winter.

Living with the Animals

Mules

*I*t used to be said that a farmer could make a living with forty acres and a pair of mules. Even within my own memory, mules were high on the list of a tobacco farmer's requirements. Certainly by the 1950's, tractors had taken over many of the tasks once relegated to sturdy horses or mules. Yet, I recall a certain resistance on the part of my father and other farmers to putting a tractor in a field of tobacco. The concern that tractors would pack the land and make it hard was one of the reasons why farmers like my father continued to keep mules well into the 1960's.

It is true that a good mule pulling the right cultivator could leave a beautiful furrow. And the sensitivity of a farmer's hand on the plow handle could make a big difference in the furrow's depth and straightness. The skill and practice that a farmer applied as he plodded along behind the mule enabled him to tilt, lift, or lower the cultivator just enough to ensure that most every inch of crust was broken, that most every unwanted weed was uprooted or covered by newly turned dirt. And there was something satisfying about walking up and down the rows and seeing the land's dry, crusty surface transformed by the turn of a plow point into a carpet of fresh, moist soil. I clearly remember the soothing pleasure of cool earth folding in around my bare feet and between my toes as I plowed. That pleasure was interrupted occasionally by the edges

This is one of the turning plows we used during the years that we culti-vated tobacco with mules.

of sharp rocks and prickly briars. Mules made all of this possible, and we took good care of them.

The first mules that I remember were Sally and Nick. Sally was reddish-brown and quite gentle. Nick was black and willful. As a team or alone, they were both good workers and must have led us through hundreds of miles of tobacco rows, cornrows, and hay fields as salty sweat drenched their muscular bodies. After Nick and Sally died, my father attempted to put together another good team of mules, but this time the match left a lot to be desired. We named the male Pete. He was black, large framed, and not as docile as we would have liked. The female was reddish in color and small—too small. Getting her to go was a challenge. Getting her to stop was even harder because she tended to run rather than walk. She seemed to only be able to pull a plow when she was on the run. It would be difficult to estimate how many tobacco plants that mule and I destroyed as she tore through the field, and both of us grew more frustrated with every row that we plowed. Swearing and "cussin" were not allowed in our family, but if they had been, working with that little red mule would have provided perfect opportunities and lots of them.

We used mules to pull tobacco slides, too. I think the mules dreaded entering tobacco fields early in the morning. I didn't blame them. I didn't like it either. Within a matter of minutes, the pullers and the mules would be drenched from head to toe with tobacco "juice." With reluctance we eased into the daylong task before us and began snapping ripe leaves from the tobacco stalks and placing them in the waiting slide. Occasionally we paused to remove our boots and poured out the water that had accumulated before slipping our shriveled feet back in. When the slide had been piled high with green tobacco, it was the mule that pulled it to the barn where it would be strung onto sticks. Occasionally a rabbit would run out from the underbrush, and the startled mule would break into a frantic run. When that happened, the slide usually overturned and strewed brittle tobacco leaves along the way, shredding them to pieces in the process.

Mules came, worked out their years, and died or went to market. Despite my intense frustration with their ornery ways, I couldn't help but feel pity for them at times. They were born into a life of strenuous and endless labor. Their rewards were minimal: a stall of their own, crunchy field corn, a pasture to graze, and a wallow in the dust. The last mules finally left our farm in the 1960's when my father decided—as other farmers did—that tractors did not pack the land as badly as folks had thought. It just made sense. Tractors could do many times the work a mule could do, and they were a little more predictable.

As a result, the mule started to decline in importance on the American farm scene and began the inevitable slide toward oblivion.

Cows

We kept a few cows in the 1950's, enough to furnish us with all the milk that our family needed. Gurnseys predominated, but we had an occasional Jersey and Holstein, too. For years we milked our cows by hand, and the initiation of a farmer's kid into milking was a rite of passage, I suppose. My time came when I was around eleven. My father simply announced one day that it was time. As the sun sank toward the horizon, he grabbed a bucket with a little warm water in it and led me down to the cow stalls. I had observed my father milking in the stable yard on occasion and certainly had the general idea of how it was done. However, within the confines of a cramped stall, carpeted with manure and rotting straw, Daddy demonstrated the procedure especially for me. He also offered a few practical tips. For my first milking, my father had chosen Lucy Jane, our oldest and most gentle, the "matriarch" of the herd. She was a cream-colored Guernsey with modest horns and tranquil eyes. Unfortunately, there would be little else tranquil about my first milking experience. As my father prepared to leave, his firm instructions rang clearly in my ears: "I want you to stay here and milk her good—and I don't want you to come back to the house until you have finished." I remember thinking to myself, "I'm not ready for this," but the job was mine to do.

As the sun disappeared, so did my father. I lingered there in the gathering dusk—just me and a bewildered old

Lucy Jane was one of the most gentle and best-loved cows that we ever owned, and she proved it by posing for this photograph with my brother Grayson and me.

cow in a smelly stable stall. Patient as she was, Lucy Jane was not pleased with my style of milking and managed to kick the bucket over a couple of times. I don't remember whether I yelled or cried as rivulets of warm milk washed over my manure-covered galoshes. The old cow and I became better acquainted that evening than either one of us had desired. Later—much later—I trudged homeward, anticipating that my father would not be pleased with the outcome of my first milking experience. The truth is that I really don't recall his response, only that a warm supper was waiting, and I found comfort in that. A considerable amount of wisdom had been added to my stockpile that evening. I learned, among other things, how to anticipate the swift kick of a disgruntled cow and how to warm my fingers by dipping them into the foamy milk. As I went to bed that night, I knew that, like it or not, a new chore had now been added to my expanding realm of responsibilities.

We gave names to our milk cows. In addition to Lucy Jane, we also had Bertha, Susie, Blossom, Michelle, and others that would live out most of their days on our farm. Then there was the mean-tempered Saulky, named by my sister. It became apparent to me that each cow had a distinctive personality and observed a "pecking order," much like chickens. One cow was "the boss," and that position was determined by several factors. A cow's tenure, temperament, size, and horn endowment all played a part. When the boss left the farm or died, the next cow in rank stepped in.

There were numerous benefits to having milk cows. For one thing, there was always plenty of fresh milk in the refrigerator. Never mind that it was raw and sometimes reeked of wild onions. Selected calves were kept to perpetuate the herd, but most were sold as veals. And there was an additional benefit. The milk from our cows provided rich cream—a considerable amount in fact, and my parents made the most of it. We brought buckets of milk from the stable yard to the kitchen, morning and evening. Mother put enough in the refrigerator for drinking and cooking purposes, then poured the balance into large bowls and pans that she placed on the old chest freezer in a corner of the kitchen. She covered the containers with lids, often dinner plates, and let them set until the cream separated and rose to the top. That could take a couple of days.

Each day Mother removed the lids, skimmed off the cream with a large spoon, and placed it in the refrigerator. When several gallons had been collected, Mother poured the cream into a metal cream can and my father took it to the depot in Kenbridge where it was shipped to the Potomac Creamery. Within a few days a post card would arrive showing the test results. A receipt from 1956 shows that thirty-five pounds of cream yielded over nineteen pounds of butterfat. At fifty-one cents per pound, the shipment brought in a check for $9.79. The income gained from all that work was minimal, but small farming operations of the '50's were not as focused on a solitary commodity as those of today are. Farm families considered every reasonable opportunity for bringing in a little extra cash. Eventually my father would purchase a cream separator, but the presence of large bowls and pans sitting around the kitchen and the skimming of cream by hand continued for a number of years.

There was yet one final use for the milk product that remained. When the cream had been lifted from the top, all that remained was soured milk, or clabber. Minus the cream, it appeared very white and had a slick, jelled consistency. We poured the clabber into buckets along with other food scraps, and carried it to the hogs. It seemed to be one of their favorite concoctions, and they greedily slurped it up as fast as we could pour it into their feeding troughs.

Hogs

Although hogs were a part of our farming experience, they probably were not the better part. Boisterous, greedy, sloppy—it all applies. And how they loved the mud. Daddy kept a few sows and a boar to raise pigs, and then sold the piglets when they were approximately eight weeks old.

I learned that hogs have very strange ways. We came to expect that a sow would mash several of her litter to death by lying on top of them. To help prevent this, my father nailed poles around the inside perimeter of each shed where the sows gave birth, so that the little ones would have a protected area next to the walls. Since rooting is a way of life for hogs, we stayed busy attaching small logs and boards to the bottom of the woven wire fences that criss-crossed our pastures. Those efforts were often futile.

Another tactic, and a dreaded one as far as I was concerned, was to clamp metal rings into the snouts of those chronic rooters. That chore could only be accomplished within close quarters, so we led the hogs into a small pen with feed or ears of corn. With a hog catcher in hand, we would stealthily ease into the pen as the hogs gobbled their feed. The catcher was a metal rod with a handle on one end that, when pulled, tightened a wire loop or "noose" on the other end. After slipping the loop over a hog's snout as she ate, it took all the strength a boy could muster to hang on while a startled and angry hog jerked on the other end. Finally, my father would use a plier-like device to clamp large rings through the hog's snout. The earsplitting squeals of those huge hogs as they were being ringed could be heard from a considerable distance. It was a gruesome task, but one that was considered a necessary part of raising hogs. The bright side—for the hogs at least—was that they were free to roam the open pastures rather than spend their entire existence in a cramped hog parlor.

We all change. Cute, cuddly, pink pigs grow up to be big, fat hogs, and there is nothing cute about them—not the way they look, eat, or smell. I learned what slopping the hogs was all about as we toted buckets filled with corn husks, peach peelings, rotting tomatoes swimming in clabber, and goodness knows what else, to the pig pen. You might say the hogs were walking garbage disposals.

At some point during those years, my father did something very special for his hogs. In fact, had the other hogs in the community known about it, they might have rooted their way to our place. Although we never had anything remotely akin to a swimming pool ourselves, our hogs did. Daddy had lost several sows to intense heat in previous summers and realized how vulnerable hogs could be to extreme temperatures. He decided to build a pool for the hogs and kept it filled with water all summer. A rack constructed of saplings and tree branches shaded the small cement pool. As the leaves dried up over a period of weeks, the old branches were removed and replaced with fresh ones. The water in the pool quickly became a slimy, red muck, but it accommodated several suffering sows at a time and helped them through the stifling summer heat.

Hog meat was an assumed staple in a farm family's diet, and our family was no exception. In the earlier years my father did the hog killing himself. Later, that job was handled by the local slaughterhouse, or "locker plant" as we called it. In some areas there would even be mobile slaughter units that would travel from farm to farm to do the job. The unit consisted of a truck equipped with a hoist, scalding vat, bottled gas tank and burners, electric saws, cutting tables, and a chill room. The chilled carcasses were later taken to a locker plant for "working up." If the owner wanted them, the hide and the head were given to him. Mobile slaughter units never caught on where we lived, and local farmers continued the tradition of doing their own slaughtering.

It seemed that there were two tests for determining whether it was cold enough to kill hogs: fingers must freeze to the bone, and breath must crystallize in midair. I don't remember the details of this ritual, but my mind does hold the image of our battered old Dodge pickup parked in the back yard, loaded down with stiff, white hog carcasses. My mother put most every edible part of the hogs to good use. There were folks around us who gladly received those parts that were not especially relished by our family, including the heart, liver, and feet. And some people especially enjoyed hog chitlings, or parts of the small intestines. Very little was discarded.

Our hog days were not to be forever. I was glad when the hog pens finally became empty and quiet, and the hog catcher was hung on a nail in a dusty shed for the last time.

Turkeys

Every spring our family went to visit Uncle Albert and Aunt Daisy Wingold. They were actually my father's uncle and aunt and lived in the community of Non Intervention, between Kenbridge and South Hill. They raised turkeys, and my mother selected newly hatched birds each spring to start a new brood. Their shelter would be a weathered old chicken house that my father had built many years earlier.

Through the summer and fall, Mother fed, watered, and cared for her brood, watching them grow from awkward, fuzzy "orphans" into proud strutting specimens. The task of caring for them also included rescuing them from torrential downpours, since they were inclined to stand out in a storm until they were practically drowned. On occasion, she saved them from each other. When a turkey became weak or sickly, the other birds tended to peck and fight him until he could no longer resist. If the injured turkey didn't have the strength to compete for food, he would die.

When November arrived, Mother began taking orders for Thanksgiving and Christmas turkeys. People called from all around the area to get their names on the list and to declare their preference for a particular-sized bird. Whether it was a ten-pound hen or a sixteen-pound tom, Mother came as close as possible to filling their requests. In preparation for killing the turkeys, my father would cut one corner off a fertilizer bag, leaving a small hole. After catching the chosen turkey, which was no easy task, Daddy would place the turkey in the bag headfirst and slip its head through the hole. Then we would head for the woodshed where an axe and a chopping block were kept. Killing livestock and preparing meat for the table was nothing unusual for families like ours, but it was a ritual that none of us kids looked forward to. Ann later told me that when she was a small girl, she would run into the house, crawl under a bed, and put her hands over her ears to avoid hearing the commotion. When I was old enough, Daddy would have me hold a struggling turkey by its feet while he placed its head on the chopping block and proceeded with what he had to do.

When it was over, Mother took the headless bird into the kitchen and dumped it into the sink. She next removed a large pan of boiling water from the top of the wood range and poured it over the turkey to loosen up its feathers. As the hot water came into contact with the turkey carcass, steam rose into the air and propelled an unpleasant stench throughout the kitchen. Feathers that were not freed by the boiling water had to be removed by plucking them out. That could be a tedious process because hundreds of tiny pinfeathers clung tightly to the skin. Finally, Mother removed the turkey's insides, cleansed the entire carcass, wrapped it, and placed it in the refrigerator. After it had been chilled, she called her customer and completed another sale. The customer went home with a well-dressed centerpiece for the holiday table, and Mother had a few more dollars to buy boots, caps, and school necessities for my sister, my brother, and me. I'm pretty sure that the sack that Santa brought to our house on Christmas Eve was a little fuller because of Mother's turkey sales.

Other Livestock

Chickens and bantams of every description populated our farm and backyard, to the pleasure of us egg lovers and to the delight of various four-legged night predators, but sometimes to the disgust of my mother. It greatly annoyed her to find her flowerbeds torn up and left a shambles by the endless scratching of her Rhode Island Reds or our pet bantams. Keeping them contained was a losing battle as they squeezed through tiny gaps in the wire or flew over the top of the tall fence around the chicken yard. Still, it was good to have fresh scrambled eggs and a nice, plump baking hen occasionally, so we tolerated their annoying ways and sidestepped the troublesome issues.

We were never without a dog. We had a succession of them—Blackie, Spot, Prince, and others that were as different in their natures as in their appearance. They all learned to recognize the sound of my father's tractor, and wherever the tractor went, they followed. While there were times when having a dog underfoot could be a nuisance, it was a pleasure to have an enthusiastic companion as we hiked through the woods or when we went to check on the barn fires at night.

And then there was "Snowflake." When my father bought a goat to use for a stew, Ann, who was about twelve at the time, quickly became attached to the animal and gave her the descriptive name. Daddy taught Ann to milk Snowflake, and soon the goat would allow no one else the dubious privilege. Snowflake became so fond of Ann that she began a practice of going to the pasture beside the road each afternoon to meet her when she got off the school bus. Obviously, there was no way this goat was going to end up in a stew. Snowflake was alternately amusing and annoying as she exhibited certain winsome traits and then proceeded in getting her head hung in the woven wire fencing, bleating her head off until someone came to rescue her.

Eventually my father determined that it was time to get rid of the goat, but my sister protested. Daddy offered Ann a deal. If she would give up the goat, he would buy her a new record player. Ann agreed. My sister later had second thoughts, but the deed was done. Snowflake was returned to Willis and Sue Cage, our neighbors across the creek. During the course of an extended illness that required my sister to miss months of school, my father walked into her room one day and suggested that she look out the window. Snowflake was back, grazing in the yard. Apparently my father had experienced his own second

Snowflake and her kids were scrounging for grain near the corncrib when this picture was taken in the early 1950's. Our stable is in the background.

thoughts. My sister had acquired a record player *and* reclaimed her goat, which was a pretty good deal. Ann could now observe Snowflake's antics from her bed as she listened to her latest Rosemary Clooney records. But that was not the end of it.

Several years later, when my father decided that it *really was* time to get rid of Snowflake, Ann still could not bring herself to let the goat go. Only when my father promised to return Snowflake to the Cage farm where she could live out her remaining days—and sweetened the deal with twenty dollars—did my sister relent. The Snowflake saga had finally come to an end.

Cicadas and Screen Doors
The Sounds

Certain sounds that were a part of my family's farming experience are preserved in my memories and closely attached to the images that accompany them. The solid sounds of an axe splitting wood bring to mind a breezy March afternoon with my father, my brother, and I cutting firewood for the tobacco barns. The garden hoes that we used to chop grass made clanking sounds as we worked the rocky soil. At other times the hum and whine of my father's tractor traveled across the fields from some remote corner of our farm. In April the repetitive chorusing of frogs and whippoorwills drifted over the meadows from a familiar pond or woods. There was the grating sound of a lantern globe being lowered over a freshly lit wick before my father headed out the back door for chores in the gathering twilight. The snapping of brittle leaves from tobacco stalks made an unmistakable sound, and so did the slapping of those leaves as they were later strung onto wooden tobacco sticks.

The droning of cicadas, the melancholy call of mourning doves, and the slamming of the kitchen screen door accented summer days. There was the ominous rustling sound of leaves being savagely stirred by the leading edge of an angry thunderstorm. Out in the wheat fields, we labored amid the grinding, grumbling noise of gears and other metal in motion as our aged combine devoured swaths of wheat. The banging sounds of falling walnuts as they hit a barn roof punctuated quiet September afternoons. Streams of warm milk emitted muffled splashes as they plunged into pails of cream-colored foam straight from the cow's bag. When autumn storms moved in, we were soothed by the unbroken rhythm of steady rain upon a tin roof. The gurgling and babbling of Hound's Creek remained a constant in our lives as it rolled relentlessly over stones, roots, and rotting logs.

There were distinct sounds associated with our home too. A rhythmic, whirring noise came from the hand-turned eggbeater that Mother used to make milkshakes for us on the hottest of days. The swishing, churning sounds of Mother's old wringer washer could be heard from the yard when the windows were open. Perhaps the most welcome sound to reach a weary farmer's ears was the pealing of the dinner bell. Ours was mounted on a tall, knotty cedar post, and it could be heard from the farthest fields on the farm. At the first sound of the bell, our mules pricked up their ears and quickened their pace to reach the end of the row. They learned over time that the bell signaled a respite for them too, which included a drink from a cool spring and a little grazing time. We headed toward the house with visions of home cooked food and iced tea in our sweating heads. The dinner bell was occasionally used to announce a surprise visitor, or even an emergency. But it was mealtime that came to be the dominant association and a pleasurable one at that.

Many of the sounds from our farming years faded away long ago. Yet the cessation of them has done nothing to diminish their significance. The sounds will always remain an essential part of my family's life summary.

Stormy Weather

Frost and Drought

*I*n matters of farming, the weather ultimately calls the shots, and the most carefully made plans can change hourly depending on the latest forecast. I learned early that weather would consistently have a big impact on the work, finances, and social aspects of our daily routines. Matters of convenience aside, our very livelihood was at stake. Certainly we were blessed with many good years and fine crops, but weather patterns and farmers' needs were often at odds. My parents hardly needed to acclimate my sister and my brother and me to the risks of farming. The risks were apparent and became increasingly clear as we got older. While they spared us unnecessary anxiety, Mother and Daddy did not attempt to shield us forever from the realities and hardships that were a part of this rugged way of life.

Our farm, which sloped toward the creek, was particularly vulnerable to frosts. When killing frosts damaged tobacco plant beds, transplanting was delayed, and valuable growing time was lost. Field corn, gardens, and fruit crops were just as vulnerable. During one late cold snap, my parents not only lost their potential peach crop, but most of the trees in their small orchard died as a result of the extreme temperatures.

Some summers brought so much rain that farmers had great difficulty getting their crops in. Excessive rains also tended to cause disease in green tobacco leaves, which virtually assured lower prices on the market floor. More often though, it was lack of rain that took the heaviest toll and really created a domino effect. Extended droughts meant light tobacco crops of poor quality, resulting in fewer pounds and lower prices. With little or no rain, even the best pastures dried up and livestock suffered. Farmers sometimes had no choice but to sell some of their animals in order to spare dying pastures. With other farmers in the same predicament, a farmer who sold his livestock during those times could expect deflated prices. Light grain and hay yields meant a scarcity of feed to carry remaining livestock through the winter.

During times of drought, I often saw my father walk out into the yard after supper to cast a glance at the sky, hoping against hope that he would spot a thunderhead. As a restless summer breeze stirred up dust and rattled the dry leaves, Daddy would study the western and northern horizons, as any semblance of a storm appeared to evaporate like a mirage. Moisture laden clouds could not seem to penetrate the arid atmosphere that hung over us like a stifling blanket. The weeks dragged by. And yet, it was always just a matter of time before the drought was broken. When a storm did finally head in our direction, the first blasts of cooler air brought the unmistakable smell of rain.

Standing at the window, we could watch the approach of the mighty drought-breaker with its black clouds, savage streaks of lightning, and deafening peals of thunder. Trees bent low under the force of the storm's leading edge. It was a marvelous moment when the first big drops struck the parched earth and pelted against the dusty windowpanes. I was awed by the power and force of thunderstorms. Early in life I was made aware of their potential to both relieve the suffering caused by drought and to inflict damage on life and property. After the storms had finally passed, we would venture back outside as my father made a trek to the rain gauge and then to the tobacco fields to evaluate what remained in the storm's wake. Sometimes we returned to the fields to resume our work. It was soothing to walk barefoot in the fresh mud as a rainbow hovered above the receding storm clouds.

Eventually we would acquire an irrigation system to help lessen the devastating effects of drought and frost. In spite of everything that we did, we were reminded more often than we wished that we were powerless to control the weather.

A Hurricane's Wrath

Any illusions that Southside Virginia was a safe harbor from hurricanes were shattered in the autumn of 1954. On the morning of October 15, Hurricane Hazel plowed into the eastern U.S. coast near the North Carolina-South Carolina border. The eye of that vicious storm swept up through North Carolina and southern Virginia—our community square in its path. I was eight years old, and the ominous talk of an approaching hurricane conjured up fearful images. I imagined a ferocious storm heading toward us with a figurehead bearing the likeness of my aunt Hazel. Nothing could have prepared us for the sights and sounds thrust upon us as the hurricane crashed through.

The storm had retained much of its strength when it arrived in Plymouth with fierce winds and torrential rains. Electric lines snapped like rubber bands under the weight of falling trees, and by late afternoon much of the area around us was without power in the gathering darkness. We watched in disbelief as some trees splintered while others were uprooted and toppled to the ground. Leaves, small branches, roof shingles and other debris flew by our windows, and lightweight lawn furniture was literally swept away. A loud crash overhead sent my father hurrying up the stairs to find that the west window had been blown out and broken to smithereens. Many roofs in the area were heavily damaged or ripped off altogether. We lit candles and kerosene lamps and waited. Night closed in, and the stubborn hurricane slowly moved on, spreading havoc for hundreds of miles as it headed north on its unusually long and destructive course.

The next morning's light revealed a savagely battered landscape unlike any seen before or since by most residents in our quiet community. Fortunately, by mid-October most crops had been harvested, so loss of income due to crop damage was minimal. More importantly, everyone I knew came through physically unscathed, but with disquieting recollections that would linger indefinitely. It was my first encounter with the unleashed power of weather gone wild, and I gained a respect for nature that has never diminished. Almost fifty years later, the mention of Hurricane Hazel still stirs up emotional recollections and remains one of the worst storms to invade southern Virginia in recent memory.

When It Snowed

Winter brought mixed blessings to farmers and their families. It was the heavy snow of January and February that stayed around for a while and slowly melted into the land to replenish vital water supplies. I was much too focused on the whimsical longings of childhood to worry with the practical effects of nature's offerings. It is possible that there were kids who grieved about missing school because of snow. But if there were, I never knew them. During the winter months we almost *lived* to miss school. And the snows came, deep and drifting. For the childish purposes of young hearts, too much was not enough.

The only sled that I recall from the earlier years of growing up was one that my father had made. It was simple and sturdy, made of rough-sawn boards, with strips of tin attached to the underside of its runners. The fact that there was no steering mechanism seemed of little importance at the time. We braked by dragging our feet in the snow to avoid plowing into rusty barbed wire fences. We sped down the sloping pastures with no thought that fancier, speedier sleds were available at the local hardware. Matters of style and swiftness were not what I would remember, but the joy of the moment and the awareness that my father had made the sled just for us. Ultimately it would be my father's presence in those early sledding experiences that left the greatest and most lasting impressions of all.

As I grew into the later years of my childhood and early teens, I began to realize that there was another side to the effects of snowfall. While being snowed in was not a major disaster, it could cause hardships for those who lived in the more remote parts of our community. When the snows piled up, my father and other men cleared driveways for families around us who had no tractor. The snow slide that Daddy used was indicative of how resourceful farmers often were. He built the slide himself. It was V-shaped and constructed of thick, heavy boards that he had sawn at a local sawmill. To make his slide more effective, Daddy added large rocks or logs for extra weight.

It is one thing to enjoy the beauty of a snowfall from the comfort of a warm home, but quite another to battle the elements when doing the chores that farming requires. A boy soon learned that having his face plastered with freezing snow and his lungs filled with blasts of frigid air while stumbling through drifts up to his waist is not as much fun as he might have imagined. But cows had to be milked and livestock had to be fed, always with an open eye for vulnerable newborns. There was firewood to get in for the kitchen stove and, inevitably, vehicles that needed to be pulled out of snowdrifts. It was not unusual to lose electric power in rural areas when snowfall was heavy. That added to the inconvenience, but folks found ways to deal with it.

Whether perceived as blissful or burdensome, the heavy snowfalls of my growing up years not only dramatically altered the physical landscape, but the routines of our lives as well. The wonder and sense of excitement generated by snowfall gradually dimmed as I moved through my teen years and the harsher side of reality set in. Still, if all my other memories of snow should fade away, I will always remember standing beside the window in our warm living room, watching a gentle snowfall quietly cover the fields and pastures of our farm.

* * * *

The blessings of favorable weather, along with the devastation wrought by savage weather conditions, continuously reminded us of the power of God. Opportunities for spiritual growth abounded as we sought to make sense of things that made no sense. My parents may have wondered sometimes why God did not intervene to spare them the harsh twists and turns of their struggles. Though I never knew all that was in my parents' hearts at the lowest points in their lives, the example of trust that I saw in them started me on a journey toward a deepening faith in God and His provision.

Lifestyles
Of the Not Rich and Famous

*I*f our community was a microcosm of the rural South in the 1950's, and in many ways I believe it was, I had a front row seat for observing it. Peculiar nuances, habits, and traditions filled our daily lives and were there for absorbing. While a few people in our area were fairly well-to-do, the majority of folks in this largely agrarian community were engaged in wrestling a living from the land. As a child growing up here, I was oblivious of the need that some folks felt for outdoing their neighbors. In fact, that need was not evident among the neighbors that I knew. We were who we were—no more and no less. By and large we accepted our time, our place, our lot. That did not stop me though from wishing that we had a newer, more stylish car or that our yard could be beautiful and nicely manicured. Like other families, we desired and enjoyed certain comforts and simple pleasures.

My mother's attempts to grace our yard with ornamental plantings were motivated by a pure love of beauty, but were severely limited by time and resources. Flowerbeds of verbena with rock borders, plots of tulips, and patches of phlox gave evidence of Mother's labors. Maintaining a clean-cut lawn though seemed next to impossible. After years of using a "powerless" mower, my father finally purchased a secondhand mower that was powered by a gasoline engine. The mower had a mind of its own as it chose which weeds it would cut. The result was a yard of semi-mown grass interspersed with unsightly weeds. That left a lot to be desired, but it was probably the norm for lawn care at the time.

The purchase of a new lawnmower, tractor, hay rake, or any other piece of new machinery was simply not an option for farm families like ours. My father's resourcefulness and patience were put to the test time after time as he tinkered with aging tractors and a chronically cantankerous combine. Daddy purchased the old combine for the purpose of harvesting our few acres of oats, barley, and wheat. I had little patience with it and felt that it came with an unwanted guarantee—a dependable promise to break down every forty-five minutes.

How often I observed my father struggling with a stubborn piece of machinery, his calloused hands cut, scraped, and blackened with grease. How much of his time and sweat I watched him pour into coaxing life from a dying dinosaur. Both of my parents developed a huge capacity for long-suffering, not altogether by choice, but because the strenuous rigors of farming required it. While I chafed at these inconvenient and frustrating trials, my parents did what they had to do and moved on to the next task.

Without air conditioners or ceiling fans most rural folks in the 1950's, including those in the Plymouth community, had only window screens to help with the cooling of their homes. Seasonal rituals included repairing, painting, and putting the screens up in the spring and removing them in the fall. The window fans we eventually acquired were fairly effective for moving hot air around, but that was about it for attempts at climate control. On sticky summer nights, it was pretty much a matter of sweating yourself to sleep. And there were occasions when my brother and I went outside in pursuit of sleep as we slapped at mosquitoes and scratched the welts left by their bites.

Within my earliest memories, two heat sources come to mind: a coal-burning Heatrola in the living room and a wood-burning cookstove in the kitchen. Heat from those stoves traveled through exposed chimneys in the upstairs rooms and provided warmth, sometimes a lot more than we needed. Years later when an oil furnace was installed, the Heatrola disappeared, but the wood range remained. The cookstove heated water for baths and for washing dishes. My mother would fill a large stew pan with water and place it on the stove before supper. When bath time came, the scalding-hot water was lugged to the bathroom and poured into the tub to be tempered with tap water. Then the pan was refilled and placed on the stove for the next bather. Although improvements would eventually come, my parents' kitchen was never to be without a wood-burning kitchen range. It came somehow to be a centerpiece for our family's most cherished kitchen memories.

Galloping Sticks and Corncob Houses

arm kids learned to be resourceful and it's a good thing, because their parents were neither able nor inclined to indulge them when it came to expensive amusements. Just about anyone who has grown up on a tobacco farm knows that one of the fringe benefits is the opportunity to have your own horse — that is — tobacco stick. Any kid with one iota of imagination could instantly transform a smoothly worn, pine tobacco stick into a galloping stallion. And, considering that a tobacco farmer's stick supply usually numbered in the thousands, think of the choices! A chubby oak, a hefty hickory, or a slender poplar would do. Endless childhood hours were spent racing down ravines and along well-worn paths upon imaginary mounts. Tired young bodies fell into bed at night and dreamed of fresh adventures that they would plunge into the next morning.

I discovered the joys of building corncob houses when I was a young boy, and by the time that I was about ten, I had become pretty adept at building whole communities of the tiny structures. When Grayson was old enough, he joined me in that pursuit. We found an endless supply of corncobs inside the corncrib. Whenever Daddy shelled a batch of corn, we would gather up a bucket of the fresh red cobs and carry them to a very special place. That spot was just beyond the edge of our back yard within a grove of tall pine trees, and it became a favorite play area in the

1950's. Corncob houses sprang up like mushrooms there and pinecones became trees that graced their yards. My brother and I cleared winding roads through thick layers of pine needles that covered the ground and built tiny bridges out of dead pine twigs. Metal Tootsie Toy cars and trucks traveled the roadways and bridges as "neighbor visited neighbor." We dug holes and filled them with water to create lakes. The dirt that we dug up was piled to form mountains. The houses themselves received the most attention, and some of them were carefully detailed. It was gratifying to stand back and survey our corncob village at the end of the day, and it was with reluctance that we left when Mother came to the back door and called us in to supper.

Within that same small grove of trees, Daddy had years earlier suspended a homemade swing for Ann from a gnarled, spreading dogwood and a sturdy pine. The pine and the swing are long gone, but the old dogwood still clings to life, and every April it showers its white petals down onto that spot. The much loved play area that we came to know as "the pines" would not be a brief stop upon our childhood travels, but an enduring haven for the playtimes of those early years. I was well past the age when most boys leave toy cars behind before I finally abandoned that cherished place.

When Ann was a small girl, my mother introduced her to the idea of corncob dolls. Countless acres of potential dolls were growing in the cornfields of Lunenburg County. There were fields of "roasting ears"—otherwise known as garden corn—and there was "field corn." The soft silks provided the doll's hair. Depending on the stage at which the ears of corn were pulled from the stalk, a corn doll might have blonde hair (tender stage), brown hair (medium stage), or she might end up a brunette (too tough to cook). Just below the "hairline," my mother and sister drew eyes, nose, and a mouth using crayons or colored pens. The ear of corn itself provided the body. But those dolls aged when left in the sun—and fast. A youthful, platinum blonde could turn into a dried up old hag within a matter of a few hours. But no matter, because there were hundreds more where they came from if Mother didn't chop and plop them into a pudding first.

Corn dolls were not the only ones that my sister enjoyed. This photograph, taken around 1952, shows Ann holding her Bonny Braids doll and me holding a toy car.

My brother Grayson (left) and I dutifully posed for this picture in front of a relative's house in the summer of 1957.

Books, Rook, and a Rifle

Reading

R eading did not top the list of things to do in our family, partly because the labor-intensive nature of our farm work left us with little leisure time. Any ren-dezvous with reading materials was pretty much limited to Sunday afternoons, occasional days of inclement weather, and a few brief minutes claimed before bedtime. We got our local news from *The Kenbridge-Victoria Dispatch*, Lunenburg's only newspaper. *The Richmond Times Dispatch* provided coverage of what was happening on the state and national scene. *The Progressive Farmer* and *The Southern Planter* were magazines that catered to the interests and needs of farm families. Each month readers found informative articles on everything from choosing tobacco seeds to the latest in farm equipment. *The Progressive Farmer* included several distinctive features. There was a section designed especially for farmwomen that offered recipes, patterns for sewing, and articles regarding rural lifestyles. Every issue showcased a new house design, accompanied by blueprints. "The Mail Box" provided a forum where farm families could express their thoughts and opinions on topics ranging from farm wages to presidential elections. Ads appeared on the pages of *The Progressive Farmer* for everything from power saws to pipe tobacco and false teeth.

Our ventures into the dramatic pages of *LIFE, LOOK,* and *THE SATURDAY EVENING POST* were usually confined to the waiting rooms of doctors' offices. Mother enjoyed the novels of Grace Livingston Hill, while my sister was fascinated with Nancy Drew mysteries.

The local bookmobile visited the Plymouth community once a month and parked in the Spencers' driveway directly across the road from our house. It remained there for half an hour or more as folks from the neighborhood walked, rode their bikes, or drove to the library on wheels. The oversized vehicle was unmistakable with its cream and green exterior and always appeared immaculate. The interior walls were completely covered with shelves that held hundreds of books. This traveling library was a novelty for a kid like me as I joined my neighbors in poring through the pages that contained fascinating stories and vivid images. Casual readers and avid bookworms squeezed through the narrow aisles and collected their choices. When they were satisfied that they had secured a thirty-day supply, they left with volumes of adventure and intrigue tucked under their arms. Meanwhile the bookmobile headed down the road to return a month later.

Big Deals

People in the Plymouth community loved to play cards. My parents occasionally gathered with neighbors at the Plymouth Community House for a lively game of "Rook" or "Setback." The kids usually went too and either played card games like "Old Maid" or "Go Fish," or created their own entertainment. They heard their parents and the other grownups call out "pass," "trump," or "Shoot the moon!" but had no idea what they meant. There were cold sodas in the summer and hot coffee in the winter. Laughter and conversation flowed freely, punctuated from time to time by gasps of surprise or delight as players slapped their cards down on the table to reveal winning hands.

At other times my parents would host or visit another couple for a scaled-down version of the community card party. The Saunders from across the creek loved to play cards, and they often visited in our home or invited us to their place, especially during the winter months. Many families spent blissful hours in living rooms or at kitchen tables, building friendships over an engaging game of cards.

Making Melody

My father and most of his brothers not only enjoyed music, they learned to *make* music. Through the years they frequently got together to play and sing. Their repertoire included everything from "Red River Valley" to "O Little Town of Bethlehem." The harmonies of their blended voices and their distinct styles of playing the guitar, mandolin, banjo, and fiddle produced a sound that belonged uniquely to the Bagley brothers. For a brief time they performed on a radio program, but most of their music making was done in each other's homes or at community functions. When they were in a home setting, the brothers would generally sit in one room, playing and singing, while my mother and aunts sat in an adjoining room conversing and occasionally calling out a word of encouragement. "Ya'll sound real good," they would say, or "How about playing 'Good night Irene'?"

The music that issued forth from those self-taught hands and voices was artless and genuine. The image of the brothers sitting in a circle, their eyes laughing, their harmonies blending, their work-worn hands fingering the strings of their instruments, remains clear and shining in the hearts and minds of the extended Bagley family. The result is that their children, and even some of their grandchildren, possess memories that resonate with the sounds that came from those remarkable melody makers.

The Hunters

When I was growing up, hunting was ninety-nine and one half percent a male thing. That is not to say that women didn't hunt. That is to say that if they did, it was not within the realm of my experiences. Men hunted—and they meant business. It certainly was not for exercise that they trudged for miles through forests and thickets. They got more than enough exercise performing their daily farm labors. No, there was game out there in the wild, and when the first light of dawn streaked across the November horizon, they were off in two thumps of a rabbit's foot. On the first day of hunting season many of those men would be combing the woods and seeking their elusive prey before some folks were out of bed. The cracking sounds of shotguns and rifles penetrated the otherwise quiet mornings of late autumn and continued throughout the afternoon.

In those years deer were animals that we only admired on the pages of *Virginia Wildlife*, and wild turkeys were seldom seen in these parts. It was mainly rabbits, squirrels, and birds that the hunters sought to bring home—and that they did—limp, bloody carcasses that were ready to be dressed. Many folks had a taste for rabbit or squirrel stew, while doves and quails were the favored bird delicacies.

My father, as well as my uncles and other men of the community, found pleasure and purpose in hunting. When I entered my teens, I was given opportunities to join them. I supposed that my father would have liked for me to, but I was never interested, and he never forced the issue. Even though no one ever put pressure on me to go out with a gun, I realized that for many young men hunting was an important rite-of-passage. It seemed to me, somehow, that this was something I should want to do. I wrestled with my feelings for a time and finally determined to follow my own path, which I knew would probably never lead me to take up a shotgun or rifle and head out with the others. It would later prove to be my brother who was the real outdoorsman in the family and a hunter at heart.

The Entertainers

The Wurlitzer

*I*suppose you could say that we had an entertainment center. It was an old Wurlitzer floor model radio that had passed to my parents in the 1940's from my mother's side of the family. The radio had a dark varnish over its scalloped cabinet and stood in a corner of our living room. It was the primary source of our family's home entertainment until the mid-1950's. Every Saturday morning Benny Goodman's "Let's Dance" drifted into the living room. It was the theme song for a weekly program of swing and popular music hosted by Bill Stell and broadcast from

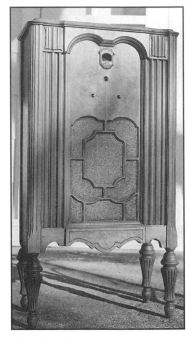

The Wurlitzer floor model radio in our living room was the main source of home entertainment for our family until the mid-1950's.

the South Hill radio station. In the evenings, with outdoor work ended for the night and the supper dishes washed, we tuned in and settled back for some relaxing entertainment. It came from programs like "Jack Benny," "Amos 'n Andy," and "Burns and Allen." My sister sometimes listened to "Inner Sanctum," a broadcast filled with mystery and suspense that gave its audience such nail-biting episodes as "The Vengeful Corpse." Our parents were not favorably impressed with that program, and I learned not to listen to it just before going to bed.

We did not necessarily hover around the radio every night, but we did tend to gather there on the evenings of our favorite broadcasts. With no visual images, we conjured up our own to accompany the voices that came from within. The old Wurlitzer seemed larger than life, partly because of its size and partly because of its ability to stir a broad range of emotions within us. The radio remained a permanent presence in our home for many years, but as the mid '50's approached, its days were numbered.

The Family Gets a Philco

It was an ordinary day in the fall of 1954. At least it was ordinary until my sister and I got off the school bus and started down our long driveway toward home. If space aliens had landed upon the roof of our house offering free Baby Ruths, we could not have been more excited. In a sense an alien *had* landed. A towering antenna rose high above the second story dormers. It was not there when we left for school that morning. A panel truck was parked in the yard. Our fast walk turned into a run, and by the time we reached the house, we could hardly speak. We ran up the steps and burst into the living room where men from a local appliance store were making final adjustments on a brand new television set — *our* television set. Could this be possible? Had we entered "The Twilight Zone" before we even knew it was a T. V. series? No, there in the corner where the Wurlitzer had stood for years, a gleaming new

Philco television greeted us. And this was not a little bitty fella, but a twenty-one inch floor model.

I don't remember the very first image that greeted our eyes from the big screen, but I do recall that later in the evening we tuned in to newscasts that somehow seemed more intrusive and more biting than the news that we were accustomed to hearing on the radio. Within a few weeks we had come to enjoy television's funny folks, including Sid Caesar, Imogene Coca, and Milton Berle. The family favorite was "I Love Lucy." Was there anybody who did not tune in every week to witness the shenanigans of Lucy Ricardo and Ethel Mertz and the frustrations of Ricky and Fred?

The generation that included my siblings and me was the first to be raised with a television around. Television heroes, like Roy Rogers, Sky King, and Captain Midnight, rounded up faithful followers from among the very young, and the commercial breaks that paraded toys and trinkets across the screen were not lost on us. Soon children everywhere, even in southern Virginia, were practically panting for Captain Midnight mugs, Mary Hartline dolls, and Rin Tin Tin rings. Countless kids, including me, coaxed their mothers to the cereal aisles of the local grocery store and attempted to persuade them to buy that certain box of cereal that held the treasure. My request was for Grape Nuts Flakes. I ate the cereal—a lot of it. But it was the plastic cars inside that I was hungry for. Every time that a new series of cars was offered, my passion for Grape Nuts Flakes was revived. As if all this weren't enough, "The Mickey Mouse Club" showed up on T. V. in the mid '50's, and kids who had never wanted to wear anything on their heads before were begging for Davy Crockett caps.

Later in the decade "American Bandstand" appeared on television, and when it came to music, teens in Plymouth were not much different from those in Philadelphia, the city from which the program originated. Most were smitten with the youthful dancers, the dance crazes, and the teen stars that boosted the show's popularity. My sister became a loyal fan and tuned in every afternoon when we got home from school. The viewing habits of my parents seemed sedate by comparison. They preferred programs like "Your Hit Parade," "The Lawrence Welk Show," and "The Adventures of Ozzie and Harriett." Something for everyone. That seemed to be the plan of programmers, and it worked.

Despite the fascination that my brother and sister and I had with this dramatic new entertainment source, I don't recall any of us developing into couch potatoes with glazed eyes and puny muscles. There wasn't time for that. There was work to do — and lots of it. Mother and Daddy were adamant that our chores and responsibilities must be attended to. This was especially true as we became old enough to share in the workload that farming required. Television was a special treat that we enjoyed mostly on Saturday mornings and in the evenings. In our home the television was turned off when company arrived. My parents would never have considered making visitors compete with the drama of a news program or the entertainers on "The Ed Sullivan Show." It would be years before color televisions found their way into homes like ours. Meanwhile we were quite content to watch Groucho Marx wiggle his eyebrows in black and white and to imagine what shade of red Lucille Ball's hair really was.

As the 1950's moved on, television seemed to increasingly influence the thinking and the habits of those who watched it. For better or worse, the entertainment landscape would never be the same again, not even in Plymouth.

A Night at the Movies

Entertainment flavored, but certainly did not dominate, the life of our community in the 1950's. Although the pace of life was a bit slower then, folks still needed a diversion from the tedium and stress that daily life sometimes presented. And an opportunity to glean a little inspiration or to have the heart lightened was always welcome.

While radio and television prevailed in the area of home entertainment during those years, movies were a popular option for an occasional evening out. Each small town had a movie theater with a marquee announcing the movie title and the stars' names. The Theater in Victoria was located on the ground floor of the Patrick Henry Hotel on Main Street. I have only vague recollections of going there because our family generally went to the movies at the Free State Theater in Kenbridge. That theater was located in the heart of town between the doctor's office and Smith's Drug Store.

Whenever I entered the semi-darkness of the theater, my eyes were drawn to the unusual lights that adorned the walls. I remember them as elongated triangles that glowed softly from behind multi-colored glass—yellow-orange, green, and red. They reminded me of candy corn. After chewing nails through dramatic newsreels in black and white, and chuckling through the animated antics of Porky Pig, Mighty Mouse, or Tweety Bird, the audience settled back for the main attraction. *Old Yeller, Song of the*

South, and *Love is a Many Splendored Thing* were among the more memorable movies that our family saw at the Kenbridge theater. A visit to the theater was an infrequent indulgence for our family. Maybe that's why we anticipated the event with enthusiasm and recalled it with clarity and fondness.

As the 1950's progressed, drive-in theaters lured more and more viewers to the outdoor movie experience. Drive-ins hit their stride during that decade and the one that followed. Even Lunenburg County could boast of its own outdoor movie screen, located between Kenbridge and Victoria. The most popular outdoor movie theater around was The Grove Drive-In in neighboring Nottoway County. In fact, it could get downright crowded there in the summer. While going to the movies was a treat, going to the drive-in was an adventure. I thought it was quite cool to pull up to a post that held those bulky speakers and have the latest hits piped directly into your own car while you waited for it to get dark. More than that, the concession stand offered treats that farmers' kids didn't get to indulge in every day.

Almost everyone—farmers, bankers, and homecoming queens—were drawn to the giant outdoor screens that were often surrounded by pastures and cropland. The accidental blaring of a car horn or the flitting of a stray bat in front of the screen was simply part of the ambiance, unless the bat entered your car. Sudden cloudbursts with deafening claps of thunder sometimes stole the show, usually during the plot's most crucial moments. Viewers could only turn up their speaker volume and hit the windshield wiper switch. All these things and more were included in the cost of admission.

The movie industry appeared to be positioning itself for a major tug of war as television entered more homes. Even in Plymouth we began to find ourselves overwhelmed by the tide of entertainment options that flooded our lives.

Music to Live By

I don't recall the 1940's, but I'm sure that my parents and their contemporaries found their life stages increasingly colored by the music of the day. While the "kings of swing" were tremendously popular in the late '30's, and throughout much of the '40's, country music was making inroads, especially with folks in rural areas like ours. It grew from deep roots and embraced a rich heritage. What American farm family of the 1950's who lived within the range of its radio signal could possibly have been a stranger to the down-home sounds of the "Grand Ole Opry"? The live performances that originated on the Opry stage in Nashville traveled the airwaves and found their way into homes from the hills of Kentucky to southern Virginia and beyond.

As enthusiasm for country music grew, a number of folks in rural Virginia, including my parents, traveled to Richmond to see Sunshine Sue and "The Old Dominion Barn Dance." Before they garnered fame, the Carter family entertained at schools and community centers around Virginia, and their appearances included a visit to our area. Mother Maybelle Carter and her daughters brought the music of the people to the people and developed a loyal following as they a carved out a career in entertainment.

I grew up listening to Hank Williams belting out

"Hey, Good Lookin'" and "Your Cheatin' Heart." Ernest Tubb's song, "I'm Walking the Floor over You," seemed to always be coming from the radio in our living room. With that song ringing in my ears, I could only envision someone buried beneath a wooden floor while Mr. Tubb paced back and forth upon it. Kitty Wells' song, "It Wasn't God Who Made Honky Tonk Angels" was a smash, but as often as I heard it, I never did figure out what a honky tonk was, and Mother and Daddy didn't seem inclined to tell me.

Meanwhile, as the 1950's arrived, the "Big Band Era" receded into the background. Hit songs now came from new artists or from those who were shedding their band image to move in new directions. Aside from the radio, the only source of recorded music that I recall in our home at the time was an old wind-up phonograph player that my parents had owned for many years. It was a console model that played only 78 RPM records. Our family purchased precious few records, but there were some around the house that included Rosemary Clooney's hits, "Hey There" and "This Old House," along with several songs by The Platters. As the decade progressed, Tony Bennett ("Stranger in Paradise"), Frank Sinatra ("Young at Heart"), and Eddie Fisher ("O My Papa") were among the popular artists that we heard on our radios. By 1956, songs like "The Wayward Wind" by Gogi Grant and "Rock And Roll Waltz" by Kay Starr were clinging to the record charts for months at a time and attaching themselves to our contemporary culture. Patti Page may have been the most popular female singer of the 1950's with songs like "Tennessee Waltz" and "(How Much is) That Doggie in the Window." One of her latter hits of the decade, "Old Cape Cod," seemed to represent all that was gentle and tranquil about that passing era. But tunes like that one appealed more to my parents' generation, and teens were getting restless for a music style that spoke to *their* generation and they got it—big time.

By the late '50's a totally new sound was taking over, blasting through our plastic radios and vibrating farmhouse windows. Even though some softer hits like "The Three Bells" by The Browns found success, Elvis Presley, Little Richard, and Jerry Lee Lewis pushed beyond ballads to music with an edge and a driving beat. My parents did not care for songs like "Good Golly Miss Molly" or "Whole Lot of Shakin' Going On." Many parents, including mine, did not necessarily approve of all that was happening on the music scene by the late '50's. But the new sound was gathering momentum, and it was only a hint of things to come. Music ushered in the decade on the wings of crooners and spun it off to the hot guitar licks and soulful wails of hard rockers. Whatever form it took, even our quiet community of Plymouth could not escape the persistent presence, and the increasing influence, of contemporary music.

White Walls and Fender Skirts

*W*hen folks talk about their memories, the subject of motor vehicles often comes up. Most of us recall with pleasure—and sometimes disgust—the significant part that cars and trucks have played in our lives. They have taken us to the work place, delivered us to favorite vacation spots, returned us to our beloved homes, and carried a son off to college or a daughter to her wedding. For better or worse, memories of the vehicles from our past can stir emotions.

My parents never purchased a new car or truck, but the vehicles they owned endeared themselves to us somehow and earned a secure place within our memories. Ours was pretty much a Ford, Chevy, and Plymouth community (no pun intended), although more luxurious makes stood in a few driveways. For most farmers it was four wheels and a transmission—definitely lower crust. The niceties of plush interiors, new car smell, and air conditioning were entirely foreign to our family during my growing up years. For teenage boys of the '50's era, the family car often became an object of affection. Even plain-Jane Fords and basic bottom-of-the-line Chevys could garner considerable devotion and gobs of car wax.

As the 1950's began, my parents owned a 1935 Ford. It was a black two-door sedan and performed every task imaginable from hauling the family to church to pulling a trailer load of tobacco to market. That car had mechanical brakes, otherwise known as no brakes at all. That fact alone was enough to make occasional trips to Richmond memorable adventures. Around 1951, my father purchased a stylish 1949 Ford two-door sedan. I was too young to realize or even care at the time, but the fresh, new design of that model helped to rescue Ford Motor Company from the brink of financial ruin and extinction. Our green '49 was functional and attractive, but stripped-down basic with beige interior, black tires, minimal horsepower, and straight shift. At least it wasn't black. My father built a shed to house the '49, and it would be this vehicle that would transport us through the rounds of our daily lives for most of the decade. This car that brought my baby brother home from a Richmond hospital after he was born was the same vehicle in which my older sister learned to drive a few years later.

As the years went by, the green Ford faded and acquired a few scratches and dents. The interior became frazzled and threadbare in places. Like other boys on the brink of their teen years, I dreamed of driving and developed a growing fondness for automobiles. I began to imagine something bigger and better sitting in the car shed. But nothing changed. Every time I went to the woodshed or to feed the turkeys, there sat the faithful '49.

In the summer of 1958, my father's brother, Uncle John, traded his car for a newer model. The car that he let go was a 1952 Oldsmobile Super 88, a mighty road machine. True, it was fairly old — six years was half as old as I was at the time — but it was a glamorous, shiny metallic green, not dull like the old Ford. The Oldsmobile had style, and it was loaded! There was a tinted windshield, automatic transmission, an automatic light dimmer, a compass, and enough room in the back seat to hold Elvis

Presley and all the Jordanaires. Most importantly, it had whitewall tires and fender skirts. When I found out that my father was considering the possibility of buying the car, I couldn't think about much else. His related comments sounded pretty doubtful though. For all the good it might do, I pleaded my case for trading in the Ford for the Olds. I distinctly remember a conversation that took place between my father and me as our family drove home one summer night from revival at Fletcher's Chapel. I leaned forward from the back seat and made a pretty rash promise to my Daddy. "If you get the Oldsmobile, I won't ever complain about working in tobacco again!" I sputtered. That would prove to be the clincher, I thought, since he had heard so many complaints from me in the past. It might turn out to be a costly promise, but it seemed worth it at the time. That night, just before drifting off to sleep, I heard the muffled sounds of my parents' voices trailing from the kitchen downstairs. I caught enough of the conversation to realize that there was probably not going to be any Olds sitting in our shed. It was summer, and much too early to know how crops would turn out. Income was autumn to autumn. Twelve-year-old boys don't cry, but I think I slipped into slumber with something in my eyes.

It came as a surprise then, when my father decided a few days later to make the trade. Our "new" car was heavier, longer, and brighter than the old one. It was only three years newer—but what a difference! The '52 Oldsmobile was all that I had hoped for and more. The extra features proved to be quite interesting. The windshield, for example, had a heavily tinted strip across the top portion of the glass. My father *always* kept one eye on the weather. When he drove the Olds out on a summer

When this picture was taken in January of 1959, my family had owned the 1952 Oldsmobile for only six months. I was really proud to be photographed with the car, but my brother was obviously focused on the dogs. Note that the car is missing its fender skirts in this photo.

afternoon, he often peered through the windshield and commented that he thought a "cloud might be coming up." That was a farmer's way of saying that a thunderstorm was approaching. Almost immediately someone in the family would remind him that clouds viewed through the windshield were—well, color-enhanced. The "floating" compass was perched conspicuously on the dashboard and could be confusing to first time occupants, especially when heading east. More than one passenger through the years warned my father that the car's "fuel gauge" needle was pointing to "E," indicating that it was time to fill up. Other folks who were *certain* that the compass was a fuel gauge must have been really puzzled when the needle pointed to "W." The automatic light dimmer was a feature rarely seen in cars of that era or in the years since. The

"Autronic Eye" was very sensitive, but undiscriminating as it dimmed the car's headlights for every vehicle we met in our nighttime travels, not to mention every streetlight, floodlight, and brightly lit billboard.

Cars of the '50's hardly seemed ready for the road without whitewall tires, and this car had acres of white-walls. I found that the same cans of Babbo and Ajax that Mother used to clean her kitchen sink were good for cleaning car tires too, effectively bleaching them to rival my best Sunday shirt. Fender skirts were the crowning glory of this car. There was something about fender skirts, and the '52 Olds wore them well. The paint job must have been extraordinary; otherwise, it would have disappeared through all the washings that I lavished upon the car. We kept the Oldsmobile for about five years. I regret to say that I did not keep my promise to my father.

Cars were not the only vehicles in the lives of farm families. In fact, they were not necessarily the most sig-nificant vehicles; often trucks were. As time went by, the farmers in our community who had made do in earlier years with a car and trailer began to acquire trucks. Those vehicles quickly became an essential part of just about every farming operation. They worked overtime and endured some grueling conditions. For these and other reasons, trucks endeared themselves to farm families.

Around 1953, my father purchased a '51 Dodge three-quarter ton pickup from his brother, Marvin. The cab was blue, while the body was black, and the wheel rims were a bright yellow. It seemed like an almost whim-sical color combination, but that was the way that many Dodge trucks of that vintage came from the factory. For Daddy, the Dodge became a consistent working companion as it replaced the worn-out '35 Ford and the beat-up trailer. The Dodge took us to the tobacco fields and to the livestock market. We used it to transport huge piles of green tobacco to the barn, or to take cured tobacco to the auction warehouse. On summer nights we drove the truck down rough, twisting paths to check the fires in the tobacco barn furnaces. Upon the wooden floor of its body, we carried ten-gallon cans of cold milk to the mailbox to be picked up by the milk truck. The Dodge took loads of dry corn to the grinding mill in Kenbridge and brought home bags of molasses-scented feed.

One of the most memorable experiences with the Dodge occurred after my parents and our elderly neighbor, Mr. Spruill, cooked a sheep stew for a church fundraiser. They had all risen before daybreak and had spent hours preparing, stirring, and cooking the stew in a large iron pot behind our house. After the heavy pot of stew had been hoisted into the back of the pickup and carefully covered, my father headed for the tobacco warehouses in Kenbridge. He expected to find hungry farmers there who would purchase trays of stew for their lunch while waiting for their tobacco to be sold. Practically within sight of the warehouse, my father braked hard to avoid another vehicle. A loud commotion came from the back of the truck. The moments that followed must have hung somewhere between chuckles of resignation and tears. The pot was overturned, and thick, greasy sheep stew covered the truck's wooden floor and oozed through cracks onto the streets of Kenbridge. It must have been hard to face Mr. Spruill with the news, but the easygoing, pipe-smoking gentleman took it well, according to my father.

Eventually the old Dodge began to rust, the wooden

Our 1951 Dodge pickup did far more than its share of work and remained on our farm for about 25 years.

floor in the truck's bed started to rot, and the tired engine developed a big thirst for oil. Still, the truck served our family faithfully as it soldiered on for more than two decades before we finally let it go.

Most remembrances of 1950's vehicles would include Studebakers. Uncle Wilson owned a bullet-nosed 1950 black sedan. The back doors opened from the front and were referred to as "suicide doors." We saw Studebakers on our Sunday drives, and when they entered our field of view through the windshield, they looked like nothing else on the highway. Watching a Studebaker pass by, we noted that the rear of the car looked remarkably like the front, sloped and sleek. For that reason, some folks ridiculed them as "coming or going" Studebakers, even though they were very popular cars in the early '50's.

Whenever we pulled into the churchyard at Fletcher's Chapel on Sunday mornings, we knew who was already there by the cars that we saw. A maroon '51 Ford indicated that the Cheeley family had arrived. The green '52 Plymouth belonged to the Barnes family, and the dark green Chevy sedan was the Rashes' car. If an old faded blue coupe was parked near the woods, it meant that Percy Bailey was there ahead of us. One memorable Sunday morning, we arrived to find a new vehicle parked in the yard beside the others. Either foreigners had come to Fletchers Chapel or somebody from the congregation had boldly traded cars since the previous Sunday. I couldn't take my eyes off the beauty. It was breathtaking—stylish and sleek as it gleamed in the morning sunlight. To my mind it was a masterpiece in blue and white, a symphony in steel and chrome. The styling of that particular model caused quite a sensation in the automotive world. Newspaper ads for the car read: "Suddenly it's 1960!" Actually it was 1957, and the car was a stunning new Plymouth that sported soaring tailfins. When we entered church, I learned that the car belonged to the Edwin Gill family, and I would have a chance to admire it every Sunday. To this day I regard that car as one of the most dramatic images ever to splash across my visual senses.

The automobiles of the 1950's were always colorful, sometimes beautiful, and at other times the epitome of excess. Some of the cars seen in driveways, garages, and backyards were chrome-laden monstrosities that required one and a half parking spaces. If all the cars that our parents drove in the 1950's did not possess style and grace, they at least had personality. They also went very well with hula-hoops, poodle skirts, and jukeboxes.

Bound for Bliss
Visits with Grandma and Grandpa Bagley

*E*ach Sunday morning as we drove to Fletcher's Chapel, I carried a secret hope that we would be going to Grandma Bagley's after church for Sunday dinner. The church was almost within sight of the farm where my grandparents lived and where my father and his brothers had grown up. To our great pleasure, Grandma would often invite our family to come by and have dinner with her and Grandpa. Where I grew up, "dinner" referred to the midday meal. "It won't take me long to hack up something," she would say. In truth, she had been "hacking up something" since early morning before leaving for church. Uncle Harris and Aunt Lucy attended Fletcher's Chapel too, and Grandma would invite them and their kids to come by for dinner as well. While my uncle Claiborne and his family lived in Maryland and could only visit occasionally, the rest of the uncles, aunts, and cousins lived nearby and would usually arrive at Grandma's later in the afternoon.

The original section of the farmhouse was built in the early 1900's as a home for my newly married grandparents, Clarence and Ida Wingold Bagley. As the family grew, so did the house, and by the 1950's it was a rambling structure that offered endless hiding places and meeting spots for the purposes of imaginative grandchildren.

The front porch swing was generally in use as the older granddaughters leisurely swung and discussed boyfriends. The younger grandchildren spent the afternoon exploring the stable, playing hopscotch on the shady sidewalk, or creating their own amusements. A huge oak spread its branches over the yard near the porch. On Sunday afternoons in the summertime, my grandfather, my father, and my uncles sat in the shade, earnestly discussing tobacco crops, the plight of farmers, a recent car purchase, and—always—the weather. Usually my grandmother, my mother, and my aunts visited in the living room with an oscillating fan turned up high in the summer or the stove well stoked in the winter.

It is beyond my understanding how Grandma Bagley's small dining room could have accommodated so many people at one time. The pine floor must have groaned as we all gathered for a hearty Sunday dinner of fried chicken, fresh butterbeans and corn, tomatoes, homemade rolls, and iced tea. We savored every swallow of that freshly brewed beverage, served in footed glasses with a criss-cross pattern. I remember the tea glasses well. Maybe that's because I often observed Grandma rolling her tea glass on its rounded foot as we sat around the table after dinner.

Grandpa Bagley, as I remember him, was balding and slender of build. He did not speak in a loud voice, but his speech had an authoritative tone. Generally, he was no-nonsense; yet, I recall occasionally seeing a twinkle in his eye. He often referred to my brother Grayson as "Grandpa's boy." Whenever we visited, we could expect to find Grandpa sitting in his favorite chair beside the south window of the bedroom. That window offered a view of the stable and other farm buildings on land that sloped gently away from the house. There was a nail in the doorframe above the chair that always held a "twist" of chewing tobacco. My eyes were invariably drawn to it, partly because its rich, dark appearance made it somehow appealing and partly because I knew that it was forbidden fruit. Whenever I saw Grandpa take his pocketknife and cut off a plug of tobacco, fudge brownies came to mind. He never offered me any though, and I never could bring myself to ask for a taste.

Grandpa Bagley surveyed his domain through icy blue eyes from behind frameless spectacles. That domain included a sizable farm that produced tobacco and other crops, along with various livestock. I never saw Grandpa operate a vehicle. Rather, he relied upon my grandmother to drive him around. She did that in an early '40's Ford pick up truck. It was faded green with cream-colored trim. With its stick shift in the floor, and spurred on by my German grandmother's sense of urgency, the old truck bounced and jolted them around for years. It was a rather comical sight: Grandma bent over the steering wheel, earnestly intent on "getting there," while Grandpa sat tall on the passenger side, placidly chewing a freshly cut plug of tobacco. The Ford truck remained a fixture on their farm throughout most of the 1950's. In fact, when one of my cousins and I occasionally stayed at Grandma's, it was that vehicle that took us to town. The Ford's habitat was the cool darkness of a weathered shed near the edge of the yard. When we were settled on the worn seat, Grandma would push the starter button that brought the engine to life, and away we'd roar. Our destination was the Ben Franklin five-and-ten-cent store in Kenbridge.

Our mission was to buy toy cars to play with in Grandma's yard. The plastic cars that we picked were well suited for our purposes. They had contemporary styling, and at fifteen cents each, they were within our budget. Sometimes we would stop to get ice cream. Preferably though, Grandma would treat us to her homemade popsicles when we returned from town. She poured the rich custard that she had cooked into aluminum molds and inserted a round wooden stick through a hole in one end of each mold before freezing. During the hottest part of a steamy summer afternoon, we would retreat to a shady spot near the house and soothe the savage sweet tooth.

Within the shade of a hickory and a large oak, my cousin and I constructed tiny houses from twigs that had fallen from the branches above us. We brought out our new dime store cars and entertained ourselves with no thought that there was any cause for worry in the entire world. The sun eventually slipped below the horizon, and the air cooled down. Grandma called us in to supper, and sleep later enveloped us. Another memorable day was preserved, secure within the deepest recesses of our hearts.

Grandma and Grandpa Bagley's house—I think of it often. I ponder it and contemplate its significance within the realm of my life's experiences. I know that I'm not the only one. I'm sure that my parents, siblings, uncles, aunts, and cousins, in their own way, have done the same thing. The unique construction of that ordinary house is so deeply emblazoned upon my mind's eye and within my heart's deepest places, that if it disappeared overnight from the face of the earth, I would still carry its distinct image with me for the rest of my life. I came to know the house intimately—every doorway, every nook, every corner. I remember what the view was like from each window. If windows are the eyes of a house that look outward upon the world, that house saw a farm stretching out and rolling in all directions, alternately yielding crops and then resting as the seasons changed.

There are folks I'm sure who cannot relate to the attachment of so much significance to an ordinary structure. And yet, I believe that there are many people who have a "Grandma's house" in their lives, and many more who *wish* they did.

Other than the house where I grew up, no structure holds as much significance and as many memories for me as the rambling farmhouse where my Bagley grandparents lived.

Bagley's Garage

*B*agley's Garage began as a small business on the eastern outskirts of Kenbridge in the 1940's. The shop was owned and operated by two of my father's brothers, Odis and Wilson Bagley, and both were especially gifted with mechanical skills. That factor, plus genuine concern for their customers, almost assured that the business would grow. Eventually they hired extra help, and the shop expanded in size to accommodate more vehicles. My uncles' big International wrecker sat out front, impressive because of its size and the bold, blue lettering on its white body that advertised the business.

The garage itself seemed to hold a certain fascina-

The International wrecker that sat in front of my uncles' garage was large by any standards, but its size was especially impressive to kids.

tion for young boys — especially those who had a passion for cars. My siblings and I often accompanied our father when he went to buy the Amoco gas sold there or to have the family car serviced. Our aging tractor received quite a bit of doctoring there, too. While our father was occupied, we explored.

Unlike any other environment within my limited experiences at the time, the shop's interior and everything in it seemed to exude grease, gas, and oil. Mechanics' tools lay all around, while old tires, dead batteries, and discarded engine parts were piled in heaps. From time to time, white and orange sparks from a welder's torch shot out in all directions, casting an eerie highlight over an assortment of mechanical debris as the odor of burnt motor oil hung heavy in the air.

One area of the shop that held great intrigue was "the pit." No hydraulics were there, just a deep recess in the concrete floor. The pit was deep enough to accommodate a man of average height and just narrow enough for a car's wheels to straddle. The mechanic drained oil from engines there, replaced mufflers, and generally attended to the undersides of vehicles. But it was a forbidden place. *No one* descended into the dark recesses of the pit except the mechanic, and I regarded it with a sense of awe. It appeared to me to be a yawning cavity that was ready to swallow up the first unsuspecting person who ventured too close.

For me, the real thrill of visiting Bagley's Garage was to be found out back — in the junkyard. That was where the treasures were hidden, and that was where my feet invariably led me. Old cars, some of them wrecked, some simply abandoned, created a promising playground where a kid's automobile fantasies could come alive. These were not just cars. These were tanks—huge, heavy hunks of cars that had once motored gracefully on major American highways or cruised quietly down rural back roads. Some of them were dying breeds like Studebakers, Packards, Nashes, and Hudsons. Some were relative fly-by-nights like Kaisers and Fraisers. And the perennials, Ford, Chevy, and Plymouth were there, too. Now though, their journeys were over, their last miles logged.

The junkyard was a wonderful place, and in an odd sort of way, it offered a heady experience for young boys like my cousins, my brother, and me. It was exhilarating to climb into the driver's seat of a Lincoln or Buick and experience the feel of the huge steering wheel in your own hands. That position offered a commanding view of the gleaming hood ornament through the windshield, cloudy and cracked though the glass may have been. Moving from car to car, we found delight in the unique qualities and peculiarities of each vehicle.

The junkyard was, I suppose, a field of dreams that nurtured our fondness for cars and fostered our interest in their design. As kids, we didn't worry much about the potential dangers that lurked in the precariously perched cars, the jagged steel, and the crushed glass. But the grown-ups who loved us did worry, and we had to leave the junkyard behind. It was with much regret that we left. From then on, we would observe the field of dreams from a distance and recall it wistfully.

Haven on Harden Street
Visits with Grandma and Grandpa Hardie

*M*y maternal grandparents, James and Lily Abbott Hardie, had grown up in Halifax County, Virginia. After marrying in the early 1900's, they moved a number of times through the years while raising eight children. By the 1930's, the family had settled in Graham, North Carolina.

I had little more than a decade to absorb the essence of my maternal grandparents' life together. I recall that the house they lived in stood upon the crest of a steep incline. The front porch and the sloping front yard over-looked Harden Street on the edge of Graham. It was a modest frame house, flanked by houses of similar age and stature. Dark varnished furniture dominated the interior, but the interesting bric-a-brac that Grandma collected brightened the rooms and made memorable impressions on the grandchildren who visited often.

Grandpa Hardie was a hard working, peaceable man, devoted to his family. He was the kind of man who stayed up all night tending to the needs of his children when they were sick. During the earlier years of their marriage, his work had included farming, running a store, and operating a gristmill near Mount Laurel in Halifax County. Those were the years before I knew him. My memories of Grandpa are from his later years in Graham, and I envision him most clearly sitting in his chair beside a fireplace that was seldom given a chance to cool. Grandma Hardie was more of an extrovert, interested in everything and curious by nature. There was a mischievous twinkle in her eye that was not lost, even on young grandchildren. She used the crook of her cane to pull them to her and smiled that "come here to see me" look. The flowerbeds and plants that filled my grandparents' back yard were evidence of her love of gardening. She had a passion for growing things and a desire to share, often sending folks home with "clippings" for transplanting. Grandma had a love for music and learned to play the piano and guitar. In the early years of her adult life, she produced a few sketches and drawings. With a large family to care for, she probably never considered pursuing art as a serious hobby, and certainly not as a career.

We usually made it down to Graham several times a year, often enough to stay well acquainted with the growing Hardie clan and the varied personalities that I came to learn and love. Uncles, aunts, and cousins never failed to gather at Harden Street when we journeyed there from Virginia. The fact that we had cows to milk morning and night required that our visits be day trips. Distance kept us from being together often, but it did not diminish the closeness that we felt then and continue to enjoy today.

This house in Graham, North Carolina, looks pretty much as it did when my Hardie grandparents lived there, but urban sprawl has crept close.

Sugar, Salt, and Succotash
Real Home Cooking

olks who have grown up in a rural community like Plymouth know that food played an important part in the individual's life and in the life of the community as a whole. Opportunities for the preparation and consumption of good food abounded where I grew up, and we experienced them to the fullest. The enjoyment began at home. During the summer on small farms like ours, families were usually together from rising time until the day ended—and especially at mealtime. Gathering around the table was an assumed ritual that provided a time for sharing, discussion, and just general "catching up" on news heard in town or from a phone call.

For those of us who grew up when fat was king and cholesterol concerns were merely a gleam in the eyes of leading nutritionists, food was prepared "like grandma did it." Bring on the butter, salt, and grease! Throw in lots of eggs and sugar, and you have the makings of what many farm families considered a balanced meal. And perhaps within that time and place, those ingredients were not the recipes for disaster that many now consider them to be. In fact, it seems that no amount of the above mentioned ingredients would have added an ounce of fat to the bones of a hardworking farm family who never caught up on their labors. Physical labors. Demanding labors. And so we feasted on sausage, bacon, eggs (occasionally cooked with pork brains), waffles, cornbread, greens cooked with fatback, and potatoes smothered in thick, brown gravy. And how we craved sugar! Unsweetened tea? What's that? Most farmers would probably have scoffed at the idea. No, "Give us big glasses of iced tea with lots of sugar in it," they would have said. And then, "Please pass the sugar bowl. We will add some more — until there is a minimum of a quarter inch standing in the bottom of the glass. Lemon? No thanks. Nutra—what? Just give us strong tea, straight sugar—bottoms up." Sugar was poured into more than tea though. Rural folks found excuses for using sugar by creating concoctions that dripped with sweetness. Tomato pudding, corn pudding, sweet potato pudding, watermelon rind preserves, chess pies, butter cakes and other delights found great favor with our palates.

Over the years, women in the Plymouth community developed reputations as outstanding cooks. But making reputations for themselves was probably the last thing on their minds as they labored to prepare substantial meals from scratch for their families. At any rate, their efforts would come to be rewarded with high praises during the prime of their cooking years and beyond.

My mother was either a natural born cook, or she acquired the ability through the necessity of providing nutrition for her hard working husband and hungry children. She rarely referred to recipes and probably only possessed a handful of them during her lifetime. In fact, I don't recall her owning cookbooks or recipe files. She would occasionally jot down instructions that someone had shared for preparing a dish, and she no doubt learned some of her cooking skills from her mother, my Grandma Hardie. But mother was more of a "taste and test" cook, using a dash of this and a pinch of that. She would have been hard pressed to write down her recipes for someone else. After all, how much is "a dash"? And what exactly is a "pinch"? But it all worked for her, and we were the beneficiaries of her culinary achievements.

My mother would not have considered herself a great cook, but we did. And so did everyone else who was fortunate enough to put his or her feet under Mother's well-worn kitchen table. Hastily preparing a meal for an unexpected drop-in was nothing unusual in our home. Repairmen, ministers, farm extension agents, and others who happened to be around at mealtime were invited to join us, and they often did.

Cooking for hired hands was an ongoing task that went with the territory for most farm wives. For my mother, that task covered a forty-year span that began in the mid 1930's and lasted until our years of growing tobacco came to an end in the 1970's. A list of dishes that Mother prepared would be endless, but there were several standouts, including blackberry cobbler. Perhaps that particular dish is especially memorable because it always appeared during the height of the tobacco season when the meadows and hillsides of our farm yielded an abundance of the wild berries. The dessert that ended up on our table was always bready, sweet, and satisfying.

And then there were Mother's memorable homemade rolls. My mind has preserved a clear image of her working the dough, kneading in the ingredients as a summer breeze gently stirred the kitchen curtains near the table or as the first wisps of smoke floated upward from our tall kitchen chimney in the fall. Soon pans of smooth, uncooked dough would be sitting on the table, waiting their turn in Mother's stove.

On winter evenings we often climbed the back steps with an armful of wood and a pail full of fresh milk. When the door opened, we would step into the yellow light of a toasty-warm kitchen and inhale the yeasty aroma of hot rolls as my mother removed them from the oven, just in time for supper. There would be butter and homemade peach preserves to go with them. When our senses had been soothed, the cares of the day seemed to drain away like cloudy dishwater.

I don't know that my mother ever realized what hearty memories she provided for us through that labor of love. To her, it was just another way of providing for the needs of her family. For us, it was a gift of the greatest magnitude, a part of her rich legacy.

Stews

Then there were thick, savory stews cooked for hours on top of a farm kitchen stove. Hearty mixtures of meat and vegetables were seasoned, stirred, taste-tested and served in generous portions with bread or crackers. In our community, the term "stew" could also refer to a significant social event, one that required planning and preparation weeks ahead of time. Within some local communities, "stews" were a permanent part of a farm family's social calendar, and they were greatly anticipated. The Plymouth and Dundas communities were known for outstanding stews and usually had people standing in line to buy.

Men gathered before daybreak to begin cooking stew in large iron pots over open fires. Stew masters of local renown directed the addition and blending of chicken, tomatoes, onions, corn, potatoes, butterbeans, bread or cracker crumbs, and other ingredients that varied according to favored recipes. Seasonings included salt, black and red pepper, and sometimes a little sugar. In the early years of stew making that I recall, the chickens were cooked in the stewpots, and the vegetables were gradually added. It took considerable time for the meat to begin to separate from the bones, and picking out the bones with tongs was a fairly painstaking process. There were invariably a few bones left hiding underneath the meat and tomatoes. No matter. That was a given, and using your fingers to pick them out while eating was quite acceptable.

Finally, there was sheep stew, with a totally different taste, and heavy on meat and potatoes. This "delicacy" appeared dark, stringy, greasy and—unattractive. And yet, there was never a shortage of folks waiting to buy, and many would attest to its incomparable taste.

By midday it was time to eat, and people gathered in churchyards, community centers, and firehouses to participate in these rituals of longstanding. The stew eaters made themselves comfortable beneath a shady tree and feasted from paper trays that brimmed with the thick, meaty mixture. The price of a stew meal usually included all the sweetened tea you wanted and plenty of loaf bread. The women baked pies for dessert that included favorites like coconut, brown sugar, and lemon chess. Stews were, and still are social events, made unique and appealing by the nature of the rituals involved in their preparation and consumption.

Church Suppers

Church suppers have always been famous for their offerings of great home cooking and notorious for their abundance of "sinful" delights. The suppers that I remember included deviled eggs, congealed salads, succotash, scalloped potatoes, country ham biscuits, homemade rolls, fried chicken, meatloaf, baked beans, pickled peaches, pickled beets, and everything-that-can-be-pickled pickle. And then there was potato salad—eleven different bowls, eleven different recipes. The yellow ones had more mustard. The greener ones had more pickle. And over in the corner, as if no one would notice, stood the dessert table. It was a disgusting display of temptations—and in church at that. There was sour cream pound cake with four hundred and thirty seven calories per crumb. There were lemon pies with meringue so high that they could not be placed near a ceiling fan. Close by sat fruitcakes so heavy that the table sagged and chocolate pudding layer cakes so rich that when served Hershey's stock soared on Wall Street.

It never ceased to amaze me how the sweet, reserved churchwomen of our area unfailingly threw themselves into dessert making with such passionate, wild abandon. Likewise, it was a given that the pastor would compliment the wonderful meal as he stood before the congregation and confessed his sin—the shameless consumption of three pieces of fudge cake. Church suppers. They have always seemed a curious blend of warm hospitality, sweet fellowship, and reluctant gluttony.

Reunions

Reunions take root wherever family life is regarded as important, food is enjoyed, and distance is doable. My sister, my brother, and I were doubly blessed in that both parents came from fairly large families. Our father was one of seven boys, and our mother had three sisters and four brothers. That meant a large extended family for us, with twenty-five uncles and aunts, thirty-two first cousins, and countless offspring. We were privileged to participate in two reunions each year as I was growing up in the 1950's, one for the Bagleys and one for the Hardies.

Although there were occasional Christmas get-togethers, our family reunions were generally held in the summer. Sometimes in a park, sometimes at a private home, these gatherings were large and lively. Hugs, kisses, and handshakes were the order of the day. Genuine expressions of love and concern flowed freely. Family news, stories, and perhaps a smidgen of gossip spilled spontaneously from hearts that had been apart for a spell. Any child under the age of fifteen came to expect at least three or four doses of "Land sakes, that youngun has grown" or "Ya'll been puttin' fertilizer in that boy's shoes?" Anyway, it came with the territory.

At some point, somebody would announce—or perhaps yell—that it was time to eat and would everybody please bow his or her head for the blessing. Then—hold on to your girdle—the real business of a reunion began. It was eatin' time, and there wasn't a shy one in the bunch. Folks representing several generations lined up to heap their plates. The reunions of my childhood did not include liter bottles of Coke, Kentucky Fried Chicken, or Zip-lock sandwich bags. I don't think this planet had yet been introduced to those commodities—not that they would have been unwelcome. Sodas in glass bottles were chilled in a galvanized tub of icy water, and thirsty souls reached for a chilled Orange Crush, NuGrape, or R. C. Cola. Ice was chipped with an ice pick as needed. Chicken was fried, not by a bearded gentleman in a white suit, but by the good-cooking aunts in the family who labored in overheated kitchens.

Fortunately for reunion-goers of that time, squash casseroles had not landed on the southern landscape, at least in our neck of the woods. Table space that might have been occupied by such alien dishes could be devoted to more acceptable fare, banana sandwiches for example. Banana sandwiches prepared and brought to a summertime reunion are very different from those prepared and eaten a short time later at home. Any banana sandwich that travels fifty to a hundred miles in a hot car has ample opportunity to ferment and become semi-soggy. And the mayonnaise of that day, unrefrigerated for a few hours, may have come close to being—oh, my gosh—lethal. Perhaps that was part of the appeal. To eat such a banana sandwich was to live dangerously. At any rate, I recall with much fondness the incomparable taste and texture of those lowly contributions to our reunion tables.

By today's standards, the food offered at gatherings of that era, especially in the summertime, was probably awash in bacteria—a disaster waiting to happen. Our current germ-conscious culture would be aghast at the food preparation and preservation standards, or the lack thereof, which prevailed during the reunions of my childhood. Current consensus along these lines might lead us to conclude that one would be dead as a swatted fly thirty minutes after eating a reunion-style banana sandwich. Yet, I don't recall seeing or hearing of any problems related to the food served there. Perhaps there were fewer harmful agents at that time. Maybe folks had more resistance then. At any rate, we came, we ate, and we lived to tell about it.

Probably everyone who has attended a family reunion has one favorite dish that hovers within his memory. I do—Aunt Susie's fried apple pies. The apples were sliced, cut, patiently dried, wrapped in dough, and folded over into half-moon shapes before being lightly fried. They were slightly tart, mostly sweet, and unforgettable.

After the meal, with food left sitting on the table, the folks launched into another round of conversation among themselves, but now speaking in a slower cadence that was punctuated by yawns. Women tended to assemble in one area, men in another, to discuss topics of interest to them respectively. Several of the women, wielding wire-mesh flyswatters, swished their weapons through the humidity-laden air, ending with a resounding "splat" on the food table and a loud "gotcha!"

The children played tag or some imaginative game of their own making. The teens tended to congregate around the family Plymouth or Rambler, listening to the car radio and draining the battery. Hit songs were hurled through the atmosphere, sometimes prompting parents to respond with "Turn that thing down!" The sight of a long reunion table, still groaning beneath a load of good food, was hard to resist. Many trekked back to pick up a second chicken leg or to indulge in another cold soda. Meanwhile, the unbroken murmur of familiar voices continued throughout the afternoon. And the older folks engaged in a sort of musical chairs, moving from relative to relative as conversations wound down and the sun sank behind the trees. During the course of the day, temperatures soared, sodas poured, flyswatters swatted, and kids ran themselves ragged. Laughter abounded, and an occasional tear trickled.

Finally, there came the first signal that the all-too-rare

event was coming to an end. Usually it was one of the uncles who announced that his family had a long way to drive and that they had better get started. As if on cue, each family leisurely gathered up their leftovers and their kids. Final hugs, kisses, and handshakes were exchanged, and unused food (including banana sandwiches) was tucked away for the trip home or, possibly, for supper that night.

Another reunion in the life of a large and loving family had ended, leaving behind powerful images and sounds that would attach themselves to the memories of all who were there. In the years to follow, the memories would resurface to enrich the lives of children and grandchildren.

Fruitcakes and Fireflies

Once in a while our family made Sunday afternoon visits in the country. As we wound through the back roads of Lunenburg County, my father would invariably tune in to the local radio station in Crewe. "Little Jody Rainwater" hosted a country music program there on Sunday afternoons. His delivery was drenched in southern twang, but radio listeners in the area devoured his homespun humor. The "Sunday Afternoon Gospel Hour" was not the programming that my siblings and I would have chosen, but we were a captive audience in the back seat, and songs like "Family Bible" and "I'm Working on the Road to Glory Land" established themselves in our minds forever.

Our Sunday visits sometimes took us to the homes of elderly acquaintances and spinsters. Their residences were often remote, and to my childish senses, their interiors seemed dark and somber—almost oppressive. The furnishings loomed massive and imposing. Windows were heavily curtained, and sunlight seemed to be struggling to get inside. I thought the hosts appeared ancient, with their long, dark dresses and austere hairdos. The adult conversations that ensued were hardly of interest to us kids, but it was understood that we would respectfully endure. It was a relief when our parents finally arose to leave, and we walked back out into the sunshine. Reflecting on those visits now, I'm not certain whether the physical elements were actually as dark and oppressive as I recall, or whether they are darkly memorable because they were exceptional departures from the brighter realms in which I passed most of my childhood hours. At any rate, my memories of those visits remain shrouded in a somber mist.

Visits with nearby neighbors usually took place in the evenings when the day's work was done. It was not considered necessary to phone ahead of time, since folks were generally home at night and welcomed company. In the winter, our parents would wrap us in heavy coats and caps, and my father would head the car in the direction of the neighbor's home that we would be visiting. No two visits were ever alike, but they shared commonalities. The opening of the door in response to my parents' knock was generally accompanied by a low cry of pleasured surprise. Leaving the frigid night air outside, we would step across the threshold and enter into a realm of genuine hospitality. We were drawn into its depth by the warmth and light of the home's interior. We knew that it would be that way, because we knew the people who lived there. We knew them to have a history of hospitality. We had seen a hint of it gleaming as an orange light through a single window while we were still quite a distance down the road.

As stars floated through a black winter sky and smoke drifted skyward from the tall chimney above us, we sat and visited. My parents and other adults exchanged stories and news. Children were expected to content themselves with whatever book or toy the hosts might bring out for their amusement. Adult conversations droned on, and young eyelids threatened to droop. We were rejuvenated when a large stone bowl of chilled winesaps was brought from an unheated pantry and passed around. Sometimes homemade fruitcake was brought out. We sat munching on whatever the host served and basked in the heat that radiated from a wood heater or an oil circulator. Finally, when it was time to leave, our coats and hats were returned to us, goodnights were said, and we headed out into the night—the air much colder now than when we had arrived earlier. The car was cold too, and the heater was slow to accommodate us. Even so, we kids curled up in the back seat and dozed as we journeyed closer to the incomparable comfort of our waiting beds.

Certain aspects of summer visits took on a different nature from those of winter. When paying a visit to nearby neighbors in warm weather, it was by no means unusual to walk there. Whether walking or driving, the visits began after supper, more often than not out in the yard or on the front porch. Without air conditioning, people were inclined to spend their evening hours outside, giving the indoor air a chance to give up some of its lingering mugginess. Gliders, swings, and lawn chairs were essential elements of every yard décor.

As lightning bugs appeared, their blinking points of light accentuated the darkening landscape, and whippoorwills took up their repetitive calls from the edge of nearby woods. The night show continued, creating a familiar backdrop for our conversations. The grown-ups conversed as the kids played "tag," climbed trees, or engaged in some other game of their own making. As the last gleam of twilight slipped behind the trees, the night gradually enveloped us all, and we strained to see each other's faces. Repeatedly we swatted at elusive mosquitoes and clawed at their annoying bites. Talk eased, and the time came to end the visit. "Let me run you home," the host would offer. That really meant, "Let me take you there in my car." The offer was usually declined, and the visitors headed back, guided by soft starlight and a sharpened night vision.

And so the visits went, unplanned and unhurried. There was a simple blend of fellowship, banter, and conversation that flowed easily. Neighborhood kids went visiting with their parents, and it was on overstuffed sofas and front porch gliders that they learned some of their earliest lessons in being neighborly.

Plymouth Junction

The Community House

*B*y the mid 1940's, the people in the Plymouth community felt that they needed a place where they could gather for various social functions. They raised enough money to enable them to build a cinder-block structure, which came to be known as the Plymouth Community House. It was constructed at the corner of Poorhouse Road and what is now Marshalltown Road. The main room had wooden floors, a large fireplace, and a small stage, complete with draw curtains. Small doors on either side of the fireplace opened into a kitchen.

By the time the 1950's arrived, Plymouth Community House had become the hub of social activity for the neigh-

The Plymouth Community House was built beside Poorhouse Road in the 1940's and became the hub of the community's social life.

borhood. In the years that followed, ham suppers, 4-H Club meetings, Christmas and Halloween parties, Easter sunrise breakfasts, Bible school classes, reunions, wedding receptions, womanless beauty contests, and monthly prayer meetings would draw crowds to the simple white building beside Poorhouse Road.

The community house became a symbol of sorts that spoke of a neighborhood united. That setting offered a place for the merging of common interests and where things shared moved to the foreground. When neighbors said goodnight to each other at the end of an evening's event, they took home with them a sense of closeness and interdependence that transcended any differences that might have wedged them apart.

The Store

Diagonally across the road from the community house stood the community store. It was a small cinderblock building with a storeroom on the front and several rooms on the back that served as living quarters for the proprietors. The Lewises ran the store as the 1950's began, selling groceries along with gasoline. When I was about eight years old, the Perkins family began operating the business, and those are the store years that I recall best. The significance of the store in our community lessened as the years passed, but it thrived during the decade of the '50's.

The store was a welcoming place, a rural oasis of sorts, in the midst of tobacco fields, pastures, and aging farm buildings. It offered a hospitable presence and might just as well have had a sign above its screened door that said: " Bring me your frazzled farm wives, your sweaty haymakers, your pickup trucks teeming with tired tobacco workers. Here you will find a place to rest, the staples you need, and the refreshment you crave." And that was true. There was plenty of milk, bread, and sugar. A massive Coca-Cola drink box stood in the corner, and it contained a perpetual supply of soft drinks submerged in ice water. The cold wetness that greeted the hand that reached for a NuGrape or a TruAde was downright exhilarating. The pleasure of munching on a Brown Mule, an icy orange Popsicle, or some other frozen delight surpassed the ability of our frozen tongues to describe.

However, an elderly woman who regularly visited the store complained one day to a neighbor that she had observed a child being sold a bottle of root beer, and she considered that to be downright scandalous. The proprietor, I suppose, remained forever oblivious of the lady's concern and root beer continued to flow freely. That was probably the sum and substance of the store's scandalous side.

The shelves on the walls of the small storeroom were loaded with everything from Kellogg's Corn Flakes to canned sardines to toilet paper. And while farmwomen could hardly have stocked their pantries from the provisions that the store offered, it was convenient to have a resource for essentials just down the road. The little store in Plymouth served not only farmers and their families, but also passers-by that just happened upon the inviting spot beside Poorhouse Road. Unpretentious as it was, hospitality was passed across the counter right along with Cokes and chips—and sometimes even without them.

Living in the Spirit

Fletcher's Chapel

or our family, Sundays during the 1950's were fairly predictable. After the milking and feeding chores were completed and breakfast was over, we dressed and headed for Fletcher's Chapel Methodist Church, which stood a couple of miles northeast of Kenbridge. The clapboard exterior of the church was painted white. The tin roof and the shutters that framed the four tall windows on each side were painted dark green.

My earliest memories of going to church center on Fletcher's Chapel Methodist Church. My family attended there until the summer of 1958.

The Fletcher's Chapel congregation of my childhood was never large, and thirty-five would have been considered a good attendance for an average Sunday. The interior of the church consisted of one large room with very high ceilings that formed the sanctuary. Short pews designated for the choir sat on either side of the altar area, and curtains could be pulled around those two corners to form Sunday school classrooms for the children.

Many faces come to mind when I consider that time and place. I remember Pastor Steve Cowan and my Sunday school teacher, Marjorie Willis. She had an engaging smile, a contagious laugh, and her eyes twinkled. She was a great teacher, but she had to compete with at least two distractions: a huge window that offered a view of the nearby road and the adult class teacher on the other side of the curtain. Visually, the curtain served to obliterate the folks in the adult class, but audibly, they were very much with us. Still, the Sunday school lessons made an impression, and it was within that simple setting that my sister and brother and I received early lessons about living in the spirit. Long before we fully understood the implications of the Biblical term, "the salt of the earth" was starting to season our lives.

Thrift's Chapel

The original Thrift's Chapel Methodist Church was a small frame structure that had been built in the early 1900's near Plymouth. By the 1950's, the community was growing, and the church needed renovations. The congregation decided to build a new church in the heart of Plymouth, right beside the community house. By the spring of

1958, the building was finished, and on a Sunday morning in June, the doors were opened for worship services.

The new Thrift's Chapel was beautiful in an understated sort of way. It was larger than the old church, but small by town standards. The exterior was painted white and four tall columns supported a wide porch across the front. A slender cross topped the graceful steeple that towered high above the roof. My parents decided to move their membership from Fletcher's Chapel to this newly relocated church, which was just down the road from our farm. New families began attending Thrift's Chapel and membership increased. As the '50's drew to a close, the church thrived.

Early on I saw that the spiritual lives of my parents and other grown-ups who attended our church involved more than giving lip service to organized religion. It became clear to me that their faith was not about legalism, but about trust in a just, but merciful, God. The Bible was taken seriously, and Jesus was preached as a Living Presence who was not confined merely to an ethereal painting on a Sunday school wall. In other words, they were not Sunday-only Christians. This is not to suggest that every resident of the community necessarily held these convictions, or that those who did lived out their faith perfectly. But the simple, yet profound faith that I witnessed in many of the adults around me hugely influenced my own spiritual strivings.

Thrift's Chapel Church and the Plymouth Community House would remain the focal point for spiritual and social gatherings in the neighborhood for years to come. Those gatherings drew neighbors together and infused the life of the community with energy and a focused purpose.

The new Thrift's Chapel Methodist Church was built in 1958 beside the Plymouth Community House.

Prayer Meeting

The spiritual life of our community was not confined to Sundays in church. Opportunities for feeding the soul were available during the week as well. Prayer meetings were held at least once a month in the Plymouth Community House. Those gatherings included folks of all ages from around the neighborhood. Even as kids fidgeted through prayers and devotionals, they were exposed to the virtues of reverence and discipline. Each month a different neighbor with a distinct countenance and cadence offered poems, prayers, and a few inspiring words.

Even reverent prayer meetings were not without humorous moments. As a young boy, I came dangerously close at times to falling off my chair while trying to stifle a snicker. It didn't help that the kid next to me might be on the verge of a laughing fit. Almost anything, I found, could tempt a kid to giggle when he's supposed to be serious. On one particular evening, an elderly lady from across the creek was leading the devotionals. Mrs. Sally Marshall was a kind and lovely woman who often wore dark silk dresses with wide collar and a brooch. She peered over fragile spectacles and kept her white hair pulled back into a tight knot on the back of her head. Earlier, someone had apparently left the screen door open a couple of seconds too long, and a cat had wandered in unnoticed.

As our elderly neighbor serenely read words of inspiration, the cat sauntered nonchalantly up to her feet and began rubbing against her ankle, gently at first, then with increased vigor. Then he began trying to squeeze himself between her ankles. Mrs. Marshall calmly read on, but a slight smile played around the corners of her mouth and in the crinkles around her eyes. As the cat rubbed, purred, and hunched his back, it was more than my peers and I could stand. We convulsed with laughter, shaking in our seats. A wave of restrained chuckles swept through the small audience. Finally the cat was unceremoniously grabbed by one of the men and returned to the outside. "Miss Sally," as our neighbor was called, ended the program beautifully, graciously, as if nothing had ever happened. I doubt that anyone else there could have maintained such composure.

A well worn, upright piano stood in a corner of the room where prayer meetings were held, and there was almost always someone present who could play it. Despite the fact that the piano was often in need of tuning, the music that came from it, accompanied by hearty singing, added breadth and depth to the evening's spiritual quality. The strains of "Let the Lower Lights be Burning" and "Now the Day is Over" floated through the open windows of the community house and out upon the night air to Perkins' store just across the road. On one memorable evening, the rickety piano bench suddenly collapsed beneath our pianist, Mrs. Saunders, leaving her sitting in a pile of mahogany rubble. Not to be deterred, someone immediately helped her up, grabbed a chair for her, and the music continued.

The songs that we sang often came from a simple paperback songbook entitled *Sing Sociability Songs (for Camp, Homes, Communities and Schools)*. The red, white, and blue cover featured a rendering of the Statue of Liberty. At the base of the stature's image appeared the words "Keep America Singing." Silverfish sampled the books from time to time, but not to the detriment of the printed words. Everything from "Polly Wolly Doodle" to "Abide with Me" could be found within the pages of those books, and there were precious few songs there that our prayer meeting group didn't attempt sooner or later.

In winter a roaring fire blazed and crackled in the large fireplace, radiating comfort and warmth to the farthest corners of the great room. An orange glow flickered over the expressive and weathered faces gathered in a semicircle. I knew those faces well, and I know now that the bonds that bound them together were meant to last for a lifetime.

Bible School

Before the new church was built, the kids in Plymouth went to Bible School at the original Thrift's Chapel. The old church stood in a grove of large oak trees, and consisted of a small sanctuary and two tiny classrooms—one on either side of the pulpit area. A curious blend of ingredients combined to make Bible School somehow different from any other spiritual childhood experience. The focus was, of course, on God and Jesus. We were taught that Jesus is the "Light of the World" and the "Prince of Peace."

Yet, the Bible School experience seemed to always include certain tangibles too, like soft drinks, cookies, and baskets made with Popsicle sticks. Eager eyes darted back and forth from the teacher to the open windows, alert to the arrival of mothers bearing refreshments to the shady churchyard. The slam of car doors. The sound of voices. The clinking of ice cubes against glass jars. Stationary tables, weathered and sagging, were spread with treats: sugar wafers, Oreos, ginger snaps, and gallon jars of lime, cherry, and grape Kool-Aid. Paper Dixie cups were filled and refilled. Mothers chatted, children chased and were chased, leaving trails of Oreo crumbs and spilled drinks.

After sugaring up, we returned to our classrooms and sooner or later plunged into singing "This Little Light of Mine" and "Zacheus." On occasion, we actually sang on key. It was not always easy to emulate the motions of our song leaders, but with energized bodies in motion, we tried. With the same enthusiasm that fueled our singing, we approached our craft classes. While there were some kids who always produced beautiful handwork and completed every project with neatness and finesse, many of us fell short. Still, when children presented the lopsided baskets, warped trays, and splotchy artworks that they had created, their parents seemed proud. I have often wondered whatever became of the truckloads of Bible School crafts that were generated in those years, since yard sales and Goodwill stores were not really in vogue then. For all the humorous moments, childish pranks, sour notes, and Kool-Aid stains, the Bible School experience planted spiritual seeds in virtually every kind of soil.

Revival

It seemed that certain essential elements needed to be in place for a church revival to occur. First, it had to be summertime, and it had to be hot—real hot. In fact it had to be sticky, sweltering, sweat-running-down-your-nose-onto-your-Cokesbury-hymnal hot. The revivals that I recall lasted at least five nights—Monday through Friday. A preacher from another church would be asked to be the guest speaker for the entire revival. Choirs, families, male quartets, and soloists were invited to render special music.

Church pews were hard and without cushions. Since air conditioning was non-existent in most country churches at that time, windows were raised and hand fans were located on the back of every pew, right beside the hymnals. The fans were quite interesting. Images on the front ranged from charming New England village scenes to Jesus knocking on a door with no latch. On the back of the fan appeared the name and number of the local funeral home ("serving since 1907") or some other place of business. When the perspiring congregation set dozens of fans in motion, the images and phone numbers began to blur. As the preacher warmed to his subject, a sea of fans picked up the tempo. Women pursed their lips and blew stray wisps of damp hair away from their foreheads while men wiped glistening beads of sweat away with soggy handkerchiefs.

Sights and sounds from outside the church walls offered tempting distractions, especially for children. Lowing cows, barking dogs, and droning tractors all intruded from time to time upon the drifting thoughts of folks in the congregation. More than that, the erratic blips of light from fireflies and the occasional flash of distant lightning tended to draw attention to the darkening landscape just outside the windows.

Enthusiastic singing, and lots of it, was a hallmark of the revivals that I recall. And we sang *all* the verses — all six verses if that was how many there were. "Revive Us Again," "Blessed Assurance," and "Just As I Am" were among the numerous hymns that we sang during revival. As the service neared its close, the preacher extended an invitation for folks to come to the altar, to pray, to meditate, or to re-consecrate their lives during the singing of the last hymn. Usually a few folks went up, but not very many. Immediately after the benediction, folks began greeting one another as nearby neighbors, relatives, and "guests" from other neighborhoods shook hands, embraced, and talked about how this was the hottest summer they'd ever seen — though it really wasn't.

With revival services ended for another year, the windows were closed, the lights were turned off, and the people returned to their respective lives to face all-too-familiar human frailties and temptations. Some of them at least, must have returned with their spirits refreshed and their strength renewed.

In Living Black and White

*W*hile growing up in the 1950's, my experiences with black families were very limited. Most of the people in our immediate neighborhood were white. However, down the hill from our house, just beyond the fence that marked our farm's border on the east, lived the only black family that I knew in the earliest years of my childhood. The family consisted of "Aunt" Rosa Seward and her adult children, Arthur, George, Norman, and Lizzy. The tiny structure that they lived in was on an adjoining farm and was built to house tenants who would help with farm work there. The house was built of logs that were covered with planks. The planks were covered with red shingles. There were three small rooms downstairs and a tiny loft-like room upstairs. There was no electricity, running water, or bathroom, and heat came from small wood stoves. I recall seeing newspapers, including comic strips, fastened to the inside walls to help insulate the house from the cold.

"Aunt" Rosa was a short, plump woman of middle age, though she seemed older to me at the time. I rarely saw Arthur or George, and knew little about them. Norman was a cripple whose only method of mobility seemed to be to drag himself across the floor from one room to another. I remember approaching the house with my sister and hearing the dragging sounds that filled me with a sense of dread at seeing his wasted legs. Lizzy was an attractive young black woman with a pleasant countenance, perhaps in her thirties. The two women worked side by side, not only on our neighbor's farm, but sometimes for my parents as well. My father hired them to cut corn and to do other work in the early years before my sister and brother and I were old enough to help.

One spring evening my mother sent my sister and me down to the Sewards' house to deliver something, most likely vegetables from the garden. As we approached the back of the house, a wide open door revealed the Sewards sitting around a table eating supper. There were no window or door screens, and chickens were casually ambling about the kitchen floor searching for food scraps beneath the table. It was an image that I would never forget.

The Sewards had almost nothing in the way of material possessions. Their lives seemed to consist of hard labor and efforts to maintain a meager existence. They may have lived their entire lives without any hope of something better. The disparity between the way they lived and the lifestyle of the neighborhood in general is painfully obvious now. Mother and Daddy recognized many of the difficulties with which the Sewards grappled. My parents also began their life together with almost nothing and lived for years in a weathered old house without insulation, running water, or bathroom. They incurred crop losses and financial struggles long beyond the Great Depression years. But they had hope that things would improve. That hope may have dimmed at times to only a glimmer, but it was there. The struggles that my parents plowed through were at least partly responsible, I think, for sharpening their sensitivity to the struggles of others, including the Sewards. While my parents' resources were very limited, and they were not in a position to elevate the lifestyle of the Sewards or any other family, they did what they could to reach out to the family down the hill. By the late '50's, the Sewards had moved away and the little house was abandoned forever. The kind of poverty that the Seward family endured was not limited to black families, but appeared to be more prevalent in their lives.

Aside from the occasional visits we made to deliver gifts and the infrequent trips that my father made to local black businesses to sell produce or fresh meat, we rarely crossed paths with black families. Infrequent interaction between the races must have made it more difficult for any family, black or white, to view issues related to race from an unskewed perspective. Strong bonds did exist between some black and white families in our community, but it would be a number of years before social barriers started to fall, and the worlds of black and white began the process of merging within the realm of daily living.

Between Two Towns

*M*y mother occasionally commented that it was a good thing that we lived close to town. This was especially true since my father often needed to get something for our daily farming operations. Because our farm was located near both Kenbridge and Victoria, either town was only minutes away.

From its very beginning in the early 1900's, Victoria's identity was tied to the Virginian Railway. It was a railroad town, and its very lifeblood seemed to flow from the tracks themselves and the trains that thundered through upon them. The railroad employed countless local men, so it followed that the hometown economy was tightly linked to that industry. The shrill whistles of passing trains cut through steamy summer afternoons and crisp winter nights. From our farm, we could hear the whistles clearly as the trains rumbled through Kenbridge. Passengers were picked up and discharged at many points along the line that included both local towns. Passenger trains made their last runs through Lunenburg County in the mid 1950's. There was simply not much demand for rail passenger service here anymore. By 1959, the line that had run through our towns for decades merged with the Norfolk and Western—there would be no more Virginian.

Kenbridge also was born in the early 1900's, and its economy and identity had always been closely tied to tobacco. In the 1950's, the tobacco market in Kenbridge was doing a booming business, and that success spilled over into other areas of the town's economy as farmers made essential purchases from local merchants. Between them, Kenbridge and Victoria offered four drug stores, two theaters (Victoria's theater closed before the end of the decade), multiple clothing stores, jewelry stores, hardware establishments, a couple of hotels, and several car dealerships. New Fords were sold in Kenbridge, and Victoria was home to a Chevrolet dealership. At that time people in Lunenburg County expected to buy most of the material goods that they needed from local merchants. Generally they were not disappointed. The vitality of the two towns seemed virtually assured, at least for the time being. Of course it didn't hurt that Richmond's shopping district was almost two hours away, and strip malls and plazas were not even on the horizon.

Our family went to town often, and we knew the merchants well. While we may have occasionally longed for something from the pages of a slick catalog or from some far away place, it hardly occurred to us that anything we really needed might not be obtained within five miles of home. Like other farmers, we lived off the land, but our daily lives were closely linked to our two towns, and they formed an integral part of our rural life experience.

Christmas

Christmas transformed the mundane into the marvelous in the world that I knew as a child. Nowhere was that fact more evident than in the small towns around us. By early December, Christmas decorations were showing up on the streets of Kenbridge and Victoria. Local merchants began scrubbing down and dressing up their display windows with bright ornamentations. By day, gold and silver tinsel glistened in the December sunlight. By night, red, yellow, blue, and green lights sparkled from electric light poles. Slender manikins were stylishly dressed and positioned in store windows to invite shoppers inside. Drug stores offered special displays of holiday candy, along with handkerchiefs and aftershave for those of a more practical mind. But the real scene, as far as I was concerned, was the local dime store.

Each town's dime store became increasingly busy as Christmas approached. They were, after all, the destinations of dime store dreamers and Santa's helpers. Shelves and bins were stocked to overflowing with any kind of dream toy that a child's heart could desire, available in plastic, metal, tin, or rubber. Marx wind-up toys and service stations, along with Renwal cars, trucks, and dollhouse furniture were part of the dazzling displays. Everything from B.B. guns to bicycles enticed shoppers and browsers as they moved past aisles of Shiny Brite ornaments and silvery icicles. Kids like myself may have thrilled over the toys on the pages of an impressive catalog, but to visit the local five-and-ten where we could see and touch them was absolutely spine tingling. As Christmas approached, it became harder to find a parking space.

Plans for a church Christmas program began to take shape well in advance of the season. Since our family attended Fletcher's Chapel until the late 1950's, most of my childhood church memories are centered there. Every December families gathered on the worn pine pews in anticipation of the annual event. Some years the program featured special music by the choir and recitations by the children. At other times both adults and children rendered the essence of the Christmas Story with a simple pageant. Props usually included a small manger, constructed by one of the church members from rough sawmill slabs, shepherds' staffs made of slender saplings bent and dried to form a crook, bathrobes, and a child's doll to represent Jesus lying in the manger. Sooner or later almost every child in church had an opportunity to sing, recite a poem, or walk up the aisle in a bathrobe to gather at the Nativity.

After the program, gifts were exchanged between Sunday school teachers and their students, and by anyone who had brought a gift to share. What began as a low murmur of voices increased quickly to an animated exchange that mingled with the ripping of wrapping paper and the chatter of excited children. Everyone received at least one gift. The small bag that contained an apple, an orange, and hard candy spoke more about the spirit of giving than the splendor of the gift. It wasn't unusual for Santa to show up after the Christmas program to distribute the bags himself. His visits were brief, and I pondered the fact that his voice sounded so much like Mr. Crafton, who lived just down the road.

My siblings and I never doubted that we would have

a Christmas tree in our home each year. Our parents had made that practice a part of their Christmas tradition from early on. We chose cedar trees since they were plentiful and convenient. They grew in profusion along the fences on our farm, in varying shapes and sizes. I gradually came to realize that perfect cedars hardly exist. They tend to be just a bit too scraggly, too thick, or too lopsided. Still, we never failed to find a tree that ultimately ended up beautiful in our eyes. We learned that even the most homely specimen could be transformed into a tree of wonder with some colorful balls, lights, and icicles, all of which were purchased at the dime store. Strings of Christmas tree lights were all pretty much the same, but one particular light made our set exceptional. It was pink, and it lasted for many years before it finally burned out, never to be duplicated. It wasn't only the physical presence of a living cedar inside our house, but its robust fragrance that brought a sense of the outside world into our warm living room. Since coal and wood burning heaters are not friendly to Christmas trees, my parents rarely put up our tree until the week before Christmas. The week or ten days that we had a tree in our house emphasized the fact that this was a time like no other in the year.

Occasionally, my father would walk out with his rifle and shoot down sprigs of mistletoe from a towering Southern red oak that grew beside one of our tobacco barns. It seemed strange to me that a parasite that thrived at the expense of its host was supposed to inspire kissing. The method used to obtain mistletoe was the most fascinating aspect of the entire experience, and eventually my brother would continue the tradition of shooting it down from the same mighty oak.

Food preparation in my mother's kitchen was probably not much more intense at Christmas than during the rest of the year, since she had a family of five to cook for, along with additional farm hands during the summer. But the focus was more on festive foods and dishes that helped set the Christmas season apart. Mother had a gas stove by the 1950's and later an electric stove, but her old wood burning range was never without a fire during the winter months and rarely without a pot of something simmering on its surface. The kitchen was hot—and busy. Mother's labors there produced roasted turkey and chicken, homemade rolls, candied yams, corn puddings, and other dishes that provided memorable meals for the family. Mother also made special candy: a maple-flavored confection dipped in dark chocolate and topped with a pecan half. She packed the candy into boxes and presented it as gifts to neighbors, pastors, teachers, and others whom she wanted to treat to a homemade gift. Christmas was also the time for Mother's applesauce cakes. They were dark and moist, and the aroma permeated the kitchen.

Although my parents' resources were lean, they both had a generous nature and liked to share whatever they had. As Christmas Day drew nearer, Mother began to prepare gift boxes for several families whom she knew had very little. She wrapped cardboard boxes in aluminum foil and filled them with canned fruits, vegetables, preserves, several apples and oranges, and sometimes a portion of homemade cake or candy. Just before Christmas my father would set out to deliver the boxes. I remember making some of the visits with him, including a visit to the home of "Uncle Herbert" and "Aunt Dicie," an elderly black couple who lived on the outskirts of Victoria. They, like most of the people that we visited, had few of the conveniences that we took for granted. They lived in the most humble of surroundings and bundled up in extra sweaters for warmth. Despite all that, their faces became radiant when my father produced the gift boxes that Mother had carefully prepared.

I don't recall the people that we visited being angry or bitter. It appeared that, fair or not, they had accepted their circumstances. Whatever feelings or longings may have resided in the deepest parts of their hearts, I never knew, and, as a child, it did not occur to me to dwell upon the question. Certainly they had never known anything different, and their closely contained world offered little to which they could compare their circumstances. As far as material possessions go, it is possible that those we visited experienced more contentment than those who were enslaved to the burdens of endless possessions. Still, those visits left a bit of a rough edge to my early memories of Christmas and caused me to later ponder the deeper meaning of the season. In that sense, the visits were a gift to me.

By early December kids were wishing for snow. We seldom got more than a dusting, and a snowy Christmas in Plymouth was extremely rare. In anticipation of Christmas Eve and the hopes of Christmas morning, the days of mid-December seemed to drag by. But momentum began to build as shopping, gift wrapping, and decorating the tree filled the week leading up to Christmas. The radio played almost continuously then as traditional carols like "Silent Night" and "The First Noel" flowed from the radio speaker and my parents attended to final preparations. After the debut of "White Christmas" in the early 1940's, more new Christmas songs were introduced during the remainder of that decade and the one that followed. "Silver Bells," "The Christmas Song," "Rudolf the Red Nosed-Reindeer," and "Rockin' Around the Christmas Tree" were some of the songs that were heard for the first time during the 1940's and 1950's. While Mother peeled potatoes and whipped up cake batter, Daddy heaped a few extra armfuls of wood onto the wood box as chips of bark and flecks of sawdust cascaded to the worn linoleum floor.

By the mid 1950's, my sister had long since discovered Santa's secrets, but for me and my brother, the magic was very much alive. From our upstairs bedroom on Christmas Eve, we heard the muffled voices and stirrings of our parents for a while, but finally we gave in to plain weariness and the sleep that our parents thought would never come. We didn't have a fireplace, only regular chimneys that bellowed smoke from coal and wood fires. I don't think my brother and I worried much about Santa getting into our living room, even with a big bag. Maybe we thought he wore an asbestos lined suit or that he had a skeleton key. There was no question that he would visit our living room. The only question was what he would do when he got there.

My waking thoughts on Christmas morning flew to what might be waiting around the tree near the bottom of the stairs. Sometimes I was the first one to awaken, and I couldn't resist an early look. Some of the packages were not wrapped in fancy paper and ribbons, but in rather ordinary paper with strings. And a few gifts were simply hiding in brown paper bags that were twisted or folded over at the top. For some reason, those were often the ones that piqued my curiosity the most.

Although we didn't get everything we asked for, we usually found that some of our requests had been granted.

The care that Santa put into choosing each gift was something that I could not fully appreciate until many years later. We treasured the toys that he brought, and we recalled them fondly, long after we were grown. My sister received a number of dolls through the years, each of which she named and pampered. One Christmas morning she found a beautiful Western Flyer bike waiting beside the tree. As she grew older, Santa Claus kept pace. By the late '50's, one of her gifts was a stylish pink and black clock radio. My brother also found a bike under the tree one Christmas, and on other years, Lincoln logs, hefty metal trucks, Tootsie Toys, and a battery-operated locomotive.

No brighter memory of a childhood toy exists in my mind than that of a red and yellow plastic taxi that Santa brought when I was around five years old. Both doors opened and when the trunk lid was lifted, a tiny spare tire was revealed. During the course of my childhood Christmases, I discovered windup cars, building bricks, a tin Marx service station with a hand operated elevator, a Golden Guernsey dairy barn, and a View Master with reels beneath the cedar trees that we brought home from the pastures. For Christmas 1959, when I was fourteen, I received my own gray and white clock radio. Current hits such as "El Paso" by Marty Robbins, "Among My Souvenirs" by Connie Francis, and "Beyond the Sea" by Bobby Darrin flooded into my bedroom via WABC in New York.

By the end of the 1950's some aspects of Christmas had begun to change for us. We were now participating in the spiritual observances of Christmas at Thrift's Chapel, rather than at Fletcher's Chapel. The powerful and profound essence of Christmas transcended any changes that our family experienced regarding those observances. In the secular realm, a spectacular new shopping center now stood on the south side of Richmond. Southside Plaza made shopping an adventure and it began to draw shoppers away from the familiarity of small town businesses, even luring families all the way from Southside Virginia to the glitter and promise of larger and grander stores. The days of experiencing a truly hometown Christmas were gradually drawing to a close for many, even for those who had never considered venturing into the world of downtown Richmond, where the impressive Miller & Rhoads and Thalhimers stores reigned as shopping destinations. Shopping patterns were beginning to shift gears, and the pace of those patterns would only accelerate with every Christmas that passed.

In spite of all the changes that were taking place, our family knew somehow that for us nothing was going to alter the true spiritual meaning of Christmas. That conviction would continue to set the tone for all our future Christmases.

A fragrant cedar with mysterious packages beneath it greeted us on Christmas morning. Toy service stations with plastic cars were among the gifts that Santa brought.

Broken Circles

*D*eath was only a vague and distant specter for me until the spring of 1956. In May of that year, Grandpa Bagley died. I was ten years old, and for the first time, I sensed a pall of somberness descending upon our family. Although I had not known the extent of Grandpa's illness, I knew that he had been sick for some time. I didn't see him during the latter days of his life, and I didn't attend the funeral. My parents probably felt that my brother and I were a little too young. Grandma and Grandpa had been a consistent part of our existence, and it was difficult to imagine that whenever we visited in the future, Grandpa would not be there. It was almost as if he had simply vanished from our lives. I could not comprehend the finality of his death and the impact that this loss would have upon the Bagley family—especially Grandma. For that time and place, the patriarch of the immediate Bagley clan was gone. The sober reality of death was no longer vague and distant. Its footprints were distinct, and its presence stalked through our lives.

Several years after Grandpa Bagley's death, construction began on a new home for Grandma in Kenbridge. Her sons arranged for the building of the house. Probably it was with mixed feelings that she made the move. While she loved her home and farm in the country, she had not had an easy time adjusting to life there without Grandpa. After Grandma had decided what to keep and what to let go, an auction was held at the farm. Furniture, glassware, metal lawn chairs, the old Ford pickup, tools, and farming implements were all offered for sale. Many familiar pieces of my grandparents' life on the farm would be taken away, and we would never see them again. Grandma wouldn't need as much furniture in her new house, and she had finally purchased an automobile to replace the truck. Her farming years were over.

My family's typical Sunday patterns, and in fact all our visits to see Grandma were quite different after that. There would be no more Sunday mornings spent at Fletcher's Chapel or Sunday dinners at Grandma's farmhouse. We were now attending church at Thrift's Chapel just up the road from our farm. Sunday afternoons would find us visiting Grandma in a new brick home that included gleaming Formica counters, shiny hardwood floors, and fresh paint. We all adjusted, but the passage of time was introducing new patterns into our lives. Grandma kept the farm for a number of years and frequently returned there to visit the family who rented the farmhouse. Gradually, she adapted to living in town; yet, I suspect that a part of her heart never left the farm where she and Grandpa had spent their married life and raised seven sons. Grandma must have missed the farm more than anyone else, but the rest of us missed it, too.

Around that time another big change occurred in our family. Grandma Hardie died in the late summer of 1959. Her death would leave a tremendous empty space in the lives of her large family. The loss was very difficult for Mother, but because we lived so far away, my siblings and I did not feel the effects of Grandma Hardie's death in our daily lives as keenly as those who had lived so close to her. Soon after Grandma died, Grandpa went to live with some of his children, my uncles and aunts. Although we would continue visiting Graham from time to time to see our Hardie relatives, the changes ended forever our visits on Harden Street.

No assemblage of personalities could have been much more varied than that of my four grandparents. Four distinct and unique personalities embodied combinations of seriousness, humor, sternness, wit, gentleness, and curiosity. The influence of their lives on their children and grandchildren would prove to be profound.

Flight of the Fifties

*I*n the 1950's, the postwar economy continued to expand. Resources, energy, and creativity were finally freed to focus on improving the quality of life for those who had endured the Great Depression, World War II, and, more recently, the Korean War. The pace of progress accelerated, along with the driving beat of new music styles and life in general. By the late '50's, drive-in movies were at the peak of their popularity. Elvis Presley was grabbing headlines and so was Ford's new Edsel. With rock music, expanding tailfins, pink flamingos, and other excesses, the icons of this culture bore little resemblance to the more reserved tones of the early '50's. These changes were only a shadow of the throbbing pace and wild abandon that would characterize much of American life in the 1960's. Our rural community would not be untouched.

As the decade drew to a close, our family was also dealing with the changes that we had experienced closer to home. As I entered my teen years, I pondered the recent loss of two grandparents and the fact that the remaining two would not be with us forever. Ann had graduated from high school in 1958 and was now attending nursing school. I had entered high school, and Grayson had begun third grade. Plymouth community was growing, and several new brick homes now stood within sight of our farm.

With the closing of the decade, the old house in which my parents first lived met its end. It had deteriorated into a decaying hulk, and my father arranged for his brothers to bring their big wrecker from Bagley's Garage and pull the house down. I was in school that day, but Grayson was allowed to stay home after complaining of feeling sick. He made an amazingly swift recovery and was able to witness the memorable occasion firsthand. Fortunately, my uncles brought a home movie camera along and captured the great fall of the house on film. In retrospect, that event served as a type of symbolic closure to the early years of my family's farm life. It occurred at a juncture where a number of changes merged to thrust us forward into a fresh new decade.

Looking back, I realize that my family and the community around us were poised on the brink of a new adventure — one that would confront, dazzle, and startle us all at the same time. Our feet were firmly planted in long-held traditions and simple ways, but we were increasingly pressed on all sides to change, to adapt to the dictates of what many of us perceived as a threat to the gentler lifestyle that we cherished.

As the 1960's approached, clear skies appeared to predominate. But clouds were lurking just out of sight. Complex patterns of sunlight and shadow would alternately brighten and darken the lives of folks in Plymouth and beyond. Time would relentlessly move us toward more revealing vistas than the ones from which we had viewed life before.

Closing

I grew up in a family that was perhaps exceptional—
not because it was perfect, but because the love
that bound its members together was tender, tough,
genuine, and unconditional, all at the same time. When
I was growing up, I complained as much as most any kid.
I longed, at times, for trivial things that I didn't have and
thought that life on a tobacco farm was just too hard. I
have long since realized that the steadfast love and secure
home life that my parents provided was the greatest gift
that they could have given my sister and my brother and
me. As a child, I assumed that everyone else had parents
like mine and a home life similar to the one that we
enjoyed. It was a revelation to me to learn later that this
was not the case.

I grew up in a neighborhood that was perhaps exceptional too—even for its time. Children like me were
nurtured by a strong sense of community. Stability and
security were the rule, not the exception. Beyond that,
most of the residents of the neighborhood shared similar
values. For these and other reasons, it would be easy to
portray that time and place as the epitome of all that is
admirable and good. And yet that time and place was not
untouched by the influences of an imperfect world.

In our present culture, "nostalgia" has become a trendy
term that implies a wistful longing for a perfect past. My
past was by no means perfect, and I don't really desire to
return to it. I do cherish my past though, and I have a

great desire to recall it — or most of it — and to hold it to my heart. I cherish the people, the times, and the places that enriched my young life and helped establish my footing upon a rugged, yet rewarding, journey.

I have used the word "tapestry" several times in this book. It is a metaphor that I like to use when referring to my own life: Tapestry, rather than photograph or painting. A tapestry is woven, one thread at a time, over and under another. The process is slow and sometimes tedious, but it results in a tightly woven fabric that does not easily unravel. However complex the emerging design may appear, however haphazardly the colors may seem to have been chosen, a distinct pattern eventually reveals itself. The knotted and twisted network of threads on the back of a tapestry makes no sense at all. But it is not the back on which we focus. The image on the front tells the real story.

The threads that were used in weaving the beginning of my personal tapestry, my childhood, were some of the most colorful and vibrant of all. Much has been added to the design since the 1950's. I don't remember choosing the darker threads that came later, but it seemed at times that they were the only ones available. If nothing else good can be said about them, they have provided depth and contrast. A tapestry, like any artwork, requires good lighting and a proper perspective to reveal its subtle meanings and true color values. I cannot change a single thread or color in my personal tapestry thus far, but I can choose the lighting and the perspective from which I will view it. This chronicle has indicated the presence of knots, tangles, twists, and turns. I hope that the images they have helped to create will prove meaningful for those who take the time to ponder the colors and touch the textures.